Sthāpatya Ved-Vāstu Śāstra

For civilized people a comfortable residence is as necessary as food and clothes. In fact the standard of civilization seems to be regulated, amongst other things, by durability, scientific plan, aesthetic construction, and successful finish of buildings, religious, residential or military. The book tries to trace the origin and historical background of Vastū-Śāstra in Vedic, Buddhist, Epic, Paurāṇic, Āgamic, Historical, Political and Astronomical literature of ancient India.

Sthāpatya Ved-Vāstu Śāstra

Ideal Homes, Colony and Town Planning

Edited by
NIKETAN ANAND GAUR

New Age Books

New Age Books

ISBN: 81-7822-042-3

First Edition: 2002

Published by
NEW AGE BOOKS
A-44 Naraina Phase I
New Delhi-110 028 (INDIA)
Email: nab@vsnl.in
Website: www.newagebooksindia.com

Printed in India
at Shri Jainendra Press
A-45 Naraina Phase-I New Delhi-110 028

Dedicated to
His Holiness
Maharishi Mahesh Yogi

CONTENTS

PREFACE

Sthāpatya Ved embraces the concept of the holistic origin of the universe. This concept envisages the view that all forms of creativity originate from transcendental consciousness. In this process it completely unites the mind and body, in the process of creativity.

Sthāpatya Ved is a branch of one of the principal Veds, the Atharva Ved. It expounds the principles involved in the areas of Vāstuśāstra (Architecture and Planning), Śilpaśāstra (Sculpture and Iconography), Chitrakalā (Painting in all branches).

Viśwakarmā, the supreme architect of the universe, is considered to be the originator of Sthāpatya Ved. Through his decadents Maya, Nala and others it has been handed down till today. Many works pertaining to this branch of knowledge originated during centuries. Some of them exist today and some of them seem to have been lost. The most notable authoritative and exhaustive text in this, that exists today, is the *Mānasāra,* the essence of measurement. According to some its authorship is attributed to thirty-two ancient sages. The other notable works are the *Mayamata, Samarangana Sūtradhara* etc.

Sthāpatya Ved while expanding its tenets differs from what prevails in the areas of architecture, sculpture and painting. It envelops within it, the knowledge of Jyotiṣ, Āyur-Ved and Gandharva Ved etc., as these branches of learning too contribute to the final outcome of an undertaking. It also takes into consideration the tenets of Sāmudhrika Śāstra and other branches of Vedic knowledge.

In this book the introduction and first three chapters are based on *Mānasāra* and rest on *Bṛihatsaṁhita.*

NIKETAN ANAND GAUR

G-1, Park Regency,
71-A, MIG Colony,
Indore
Phone: (0731) 543516
E-mail: vedicvastu@hotmail.com

INTRODUCTION*

HISTORICAL BACKGROUND

For civilized people a comfortable residence is as necessary as food and clothes. In fact the standard of civilization seems to be regulated, amongst other things, by durability, scientific plan, aesthetic construction, and successful finish of buildings, religious, residential or military. It is, therefore, not surprising to find references to the art of building in all branches of the literature of a cultured people. For ancient Indian writers, at any rate, architecture seems to have been a very fascinating subject, inasmuch as the Vedic, Buddhist, Epic, Paurāṇic, Āgamic, Historical, Political and even Astronomical literature bear traces of it. We refer here briefly the representative branches of literature.

I Vedic Literature

It is needless to say that the details of the art of building were systematically embodied for the first time in the avowedly architectural treatises. They are necessarily missing in non-architectural literature, especially that composed before the growth of the *Vāstu-śāstras.* But casual references to this art go as far back as the oldest existing literature of the world. The Vedic literature before the Sūtra period, however, contains little about the structure of a house. That the people of that time had learnt the art of building and used to reside in constructed houses and not in caves is sufficiently clear, not only from the synonyms for a house but also from the component members of a building, such as doors, pillars, and crossbeams. "The hymns of the Atharva-veda give some information about the construction of a house, but the details are extremely obscure......... According to Zimmer, four pillars (*upamit*) were set up on a good site, and against them beams were leant at an angle as props (*pratimit*). The upright pillars were connected by crossbeams (*parimit*) resting upon them. The roof was formed of ribs of bamboo cane (*vaṁśa*), ... The walls were filled up with

* Reproduced in an extract form from *Manasara,* Volume II: "Indian Architecture", pp. 5-33

grass in bundles (*palada*), and the whole structure was held together by ties of various sorts (*nahana, prāṇāha, saṁdaṁśa, parishvañjalya*). It was composed of several rooms, ..., and it could be securely shut up."

Atri is stated to have been "thrown into a machine room with a hundred doors, where he was roasted."? Vasiṣṭha desired to have "a three-storeyed dwelling" (*tri-dhātu-śaraṇam*). Mention is made of a sovereign "who, exercising no oppression, sits down in this substantial and elegant hall built with a thousand pillars," and of residential houses with such pillars as are said to be "vast, comprehensive, and thousand-doored. Mitra and Varuṇa are represented as occupying a great palace with a thousand pillars and a thousand gates. Muir is quite reasonable when he comments on this by saying that "this is but an exaggerated description of a royal residence such as the poet had seen.

The *Śulva-Sūtras,* which are but the supplementary portions of the *Kalpa-Sūtras,* treating of the measurement and construction of the different *Vedis* or altars, furnish us with some interesting structural details of the Agnis, the large altars built of bricks. The construction of these altars, which were required for the great Soma sacrifice, seems to have been based on sound scientific principles and was probably the beginning of religious architecture (temple-building) in India.

These altars could be constructed in different shapes, the earliest enumeration of which is found in the *Taittirīya-Saṁhitā.* Following this enumeration, Baudhāyans and Āpastamba furnish us with full particulars about the shape of all these different *chitis* (altars) and the bricks which were employed for their construction. Everyone of these altars was constructed of five layers of bricks, which together came up to the height of the knee; in some cases 10 or 15 layers, and proportionate increase in the height of the altar were prescribed. Every layer in its turn was to consist of two hundred bricks, so that the whole *Agni* (altar) contained a thousand ; the first, third, and fifth layers were divided into two hundred parts in exactly the same manner ; a different division was adopted for the second and the fourth, so that one brick was never laid upon another of the same size and form.

"The first altar covered an area of 7½ *puruṣas,* which means 7½ squares, each side of which was equal to a *puruṣa,* i.e., the height of a man with uplifted arms. On each subsequent occasion the area was increased by one square *puruṣa.* Thus, at the second layer of the altar one square *puruṣa* was added to the 7½ constituting the first *chiti* (altar), and at the third layer two square *puruṣas* were added and so on. But the shape of the whole and the relative proportion of each constituent part had to remain unchanged. The area of every *chiti* (altar), whatever its shape might be—falcon, wheel tortoise, etc.,—had to be equal to 7½ square *puruṣas.*

Frequent mention is made also of villages towns and forts, and cities with hundred enclosures or fortifications are referred to. On this Muir remarks that although they are only alluded to as figurative expressions of the means of protection afforded by the gods, they no doubt suggest the idea of forts consisting apparently of a series of concentric walls, as actually existing in the country at that time."

From references like these many scholars are of opinion that the authors of the Vedic literature "were not ignorant of stone forts, walled cities, stone houses, carved stones, and brick edifices."

II Buddhist Literature

"In the Buddha's time and in that portion of northern India where the Buddhist influence was most early felt—that is to say, in the districts including and adjoining those now called the United Provinces and Behar"—the arrangements of villages were practically similar, "We nowhere hear of isolated houses. The houses were all together, in a group, separated only by narrow lanes. Immediately adjoining was the sacred grove of trees of the primeval forest ...... Beyond this was the wide expanse of cultivated field, usually rice field." Villagers are described as "uniting of their own accord to build mote-hills and rest-houses and reservoirs, to mend the roads between their own and adjacent villages, and even to lay out parks."

The exact details of town-planning are not available. But "we are told of lofty walls, ramparts with buttresses and watch-towers and great gates ; the whole surrounded by a moat or even a double moat, one of water and one of mud. But we are nowhere told of the length of the fortifications or of the extent of the space they enclosed. It would seem that we have to think not so much of a large walled city as of a fort surrounded by a number of suburbs ...... From the frequent mention of the windows of the great houses opening directly on to the streets or squares it would appear that it was not the custom to have them surrounded by any private grounds. There were, however, no doubt, enclosed spaces behind the fronts of the houses, which latter abutted on the streets."

But detached references to individual buildings, as distinct from villages and towns, are found in abundance in the canonical texts as well as the Jātakas. At places it appears as if Buddha were delivering discourses on architecture. As a matter of fact, he enjoined upon his devotees the supervision of building construction as one of the duties of the order. It is stated in one of the early texts that the Bhikkhus were told on a certain occasion by the Blessed One, after the delivery of a religious discourse, with respect to dwellings, thus : 'I allow you O Bhikkhus, abodes of five kinds—*Vihāra, Arddhayoga, Prāsāda, Harmya, and Guhā.'*

Buildings are thus divided into five classes. But the details of the distinguishing features are not methodically given in the texts, obviously because these are not architectural treatises.

Vihāras are the well-known monasteries or temples of the Buddhists, originally implying halls where the monks met. *Adhayogas* seem to be a special kind of Bengal buildings, partly religious and partly residential. *Prāsādas* are wholly residential storeyed buildings ; *Harmyas* are a larger and more pompous type of storeyed buildings. *Guhās* seem to be less dignified buildings, originally built underground for middle-class people. The extensiveness of these buildings can be imagined from the length of time devoted to getting a house completely built. Thus, it is stated that "with reference to the work of a small *Vihāra,* is may be given in charge (to an overseer) as a *Navakamma* (new work) for a period of five or six years, that on an *Aḍḍhayoga* for a period of seven or eight years, that on a large *Vihāra* or *a Pāsāda* for ten or twelve years." That the long periods were not idled away will be clear from the following details of houses gathered from the Vinaya texts.

The selection of building sites shows a highly developed good taste. The *ārāma* (rest-house), well fitted for quiet people, is stated to be built "not too far from the town and not too near, convenient for going and for coming, easily accessible for all who wish to visit him, by day not too crowded, by night not exposed to too much noise and alarm ...." The whole compound is enclosed with ramparts (*prākāra*) of three kinds, namely, brick walls, stone walls, and wooden fences, which are again surrounded with bamboo fences, thorn fences, and ditches.

Houses were built comprising "dwelling-rooms and retiring-rooms, and store-rooms, and service halls and halls with fire-places in them, and store-houses,, and closets, and cloisters, and halls for exercise, and wells, and sheds for the well, and bath-rooms, and halls attached to the bath-rooms, and ponds, and open-roofed sheds (maṇḍapas)." These buildings are meant to be dwelling houses ; so it is stated that "an *upāsaka* (devotee) has built for his own use a residence, a sleeping room, a stable, a tower, a one-peaked building, a shop, *a boutique,* a storeyed house, an attic, a cave, a cell, a store-room, a refectory, a fire-room, a kitchen, a privy, a place to walk in, a house to walk in, a well, a well-house, a *yantra-gṛha* (which is supposed by Būhler to be 'a bathing place for hot sitting baths'), a *yantra-gṛha* room, a lotus pond and a pavilion."

The inner chambers are divided into three classes, called *Śivikā-garbha* or square halls, *Nālikā-garbha* or rectangular halls, and *Harmya-garbha* which appears to be a large dining-hall. The verandahs (*alinda*) seem to have been a special characteristic of these buildings. The Blessed One (Buddha) says, "I allow you, O Bhikkhus, covered terraces, inner verandahs, and over-hanging caves." The storeyed buildings (*prāsāda*) are stated to be furnished with "a verandah to it, supported on pillars" with capitals of elephant-head.

Details of gates, doors and windows are also elaborate. Gateways are built with rooms and ornamental screen-work over them. And gates are made of stakes interlaced with thorny brakes.

Doors are furnished with "door-posts and lintel, with hollows like a mortar for the door to revolve in, with projections to revolve in those hollows, with rings on the door for the bolt to work along in, with a block of wood fixed into the edge of the door-post, and containing a cavity for the bolt to go into (called the monkey's head), with a pin to secure the bolt by, with a connecting bolt, with a key-hole, with a hole for a string with which the door may be closed, and with a string for that purpose. The windows are stated to be of three kinds according as they are made with railings, lattices, and slips of wood. The shutters are adjustable and can be closed or opened whenever required. Five kinds of roofing are mentioned—brick-roofing, stone-roofing, cement-roofing, straw-roofing, and roofing of leaves. The roof is first covered over with skins (?) and plastered within and without ; then follow whitewash, blocking, red-colouring, wreath-work and creeper-work. "The floors were of earth, not of wood, and were restored from time to time by fresh clay or dry cowdung being laid down, and then covered with a whitewash in which sometimes black or red was mixed. From the parallel passage in *Mahāvagga* (I.25. 15) and *Chullavagga* (VIII. 3.I), it would seem that the red colouring was used rather for walls, and the black one for floors." It appears, however, that with a view to removing the dampness gravel was spread over the floor.

There were stairs of three kinds, namely brick stairs, stone stairs, and wooden stairs. And they were furnished with *ālambana-bāhu* or balustrades. A more detailed description of flights of stairs (*sopāna*) is given in the *Mahā-Sudassana Sutta* : "Each of these had a *thambhā,* evidently posts or banisters ; *sūchiyo,* apparently cross-bars let into these banisters; and *uṇhīsaṁ,* either a head-line running along the top of the banisters, or a figure-head at the lower end of such a head-line."

Thus it is clear that very minute details also are mentioned in this literature. The subject, therefore, seems to have been treated in a more than casual manner.

"The entrance to the great houses was through a large gateway. To the right and left of the passage-way were the treasury and grain stores. The gateway led into an inner courtyard round which were chambers on the ground floor. And above these chambers was a flat roof called the *upari-prāsāda tala,* the upper flat surface of the house, where the owner sat, usually under a pavilion which answered the purpose at once of a drawing-room, an office, and a dining-hall."

"In the King's palace there was accommodation also for all the business of the state, and for the numerous retinue and the extensive harem.......... The supplementary buildings included three institutions which are strange to us, and of considerable historical interest."

"We are told several times of a building of seven storeys in height." Professor Rhys Davids seems to be of the opinion that these buildings must have some connection with the seven-storyed Ziggarats of Chaldaea. "But in India the use to which such seven-storeyed palaces were put was entirely private, and had nothing to do with any worship of the stars." Still he would add that "in this case also the Indians were borrowers of an idea."

"Another sort of building historically interesting were the hot-air baths, described in full in *Vinaya texts.* They were built on an elevated basement faced with brick or stone, with stone stairs leading up to it, and a railing round the verandah. The roof and walls were of wood, covered first with skins, and then with plaster ; the lower part only of the wall being faced with bricks. There was an ante-chamber, and a hot-room, and a pool to bathe in. Seats were arranged round a fire-place in the middle of the hot room ; and to induce perspiration hot water was poured over the bathers................."

In the *Dīgha Nikāya* there is a description of "another sort of bath, an open air bathing tank, with flights of steps leading to it, faced entirely with stone, and ornamented both with flowers and carvings."

The Dāgabas or topes were another class of monuments erected in the cemeteries. They were pre-Buddhistic in origin but became very prominent after Buddha. The priestly records, however, ignore these topes, because they were erected "more especially by those who had thrown off their allegiance to the priests, and were desirous to honour the memory of their teachers, who were leaders of thought, or reformers, or philosophers."

"The first step was probably merely to build the cairn more carefully than usual with stones and to cover the outside with fine *chunam* plaster to give a marble-like surface. The next step was to build the cairn of concentric layers of the huge bricks in use at the time, and to surround the whole with a wooden railing."

"Even in the Buddha's time the size of these monuments had already reached very considerable dimensions. The solid dome erected by the Sākiyas over their share of the ashes from the Buddha's funeral pyre must have been about the same height as the dome of the St. Paul's measured from the roof."

From the books referring to the earlier Buddhist period stone seems to have been used only for pillars, walls and stair cases. A palace of stone is once mentioned in a fairy land. According to Rhys Davids, "the superstructure at least, of all dwellings was either of woodwork or brickwork. In either case it was often covered, both internally and externally, with fine chunam plaster-works, and brilliantly painted in fresco, with figures or patterns, four of which have been preserved, namely, wreath-work, creeper-work, fine-ribbon-work and dragon's-tooth-work. When the figures predominated the result is often called a picture-gallery (*chittāgāra*).

The articles of furniture, which form an important part of the architectural subjects, are also elaborately described in the Buddhist literature. Benches were made long enough to accommodate three persons'. The bedstead (*pallaṅka*) or divan was a separate piece of furniture. Large couches (*āsandi*) or chairs seem to have been important articles of furniture. Couches covered with canopies are also mentioned. Mention is made of a large variety of chairs, namely, rectangular chair (*āsandako*), arm chair, sofa (*sattaṅgo*), sofa with arms to it, state chair (*bhadda-pīṭham*), cushioned chair (*pīṭhikā*), chair raised on a pedestal *etaka-padaka-pīḷham*), chair with many legs (*āmalaka-vaṇṭika-pīṭham*), leaning board (*phalakam*), cane-bottomed chair (*Koccham*) and straw-bottomed chair. Mention is also made of the litter or sedan-chair.

Valuable carpets, rugs, pillows, curtains, and such other luxurious decorations also are elaborately described. Thus mention is made of "coverlets with long fleece, counterpanes of many colours, woollen coverlets white or marked with thick flowers, mattresses, cotton coverlets dyed with figures of animals, rugs with long hair on one or both sides, carpets inwrought with gold or with silk, large woollen carpets such as the nautch (dancing) girls dance upon, rich elephant housings, horse rugs or carriage rugs, panther or antelope skins, large cushions and crimson cushions. Pillows are of various kinds ; they are stated to be of both "the size of a man's head" and halt "the size of a man's body." The Buddha allows the Bhikkhus "to comb out the cotton, and make the cotton up into pillows if it be of any of these three kinds, cotton produced on trees, cotton produced on creepers, and cotton produced from *potaki-grass.*" The bolsters made for the use of high officials were of five kinds as they were stuffed with wool, cotton cloth, bark, grass or leaves. There were also coverlets for them. The smaller articles like the floor cloth, mosquito curtain, handkerchief and spittoon did not escape the notice of the then house-decorators."

III Classical Literature

The Epics

The Epics furnish copious description of cities, storeyed buildings, balconies porticos, triumphal arches, enclosing walls, flights of stone masonry steps for tanks and a variety of other structures, all indicative of a flourishing architecture in the country.

The plan of the city of Ayodhyā is strikingly similar to the town-plan given in the *Mānasāra* and other architectural treatises. "The temples (*devāyatana*) in this city (Ayodhyā) were as resplendent as the sky. Its assembly-halls, gardens, and alms-houses (*prapā*) were most elegant ; and everywhere were arranged extensive buildings crowded with men and women........ The houses were as mines of gems, and the abodes of the goddess of fortune. The steeples (*śikhara*) of the houses were as resplendent as the crests of mountains and bore hundreds of pavilions (*vimāna*) like the celestial palace of the chief among the Devas. The rooms were full of riches and corn, exquisitely gilt and decorated, and seemed as charming as pictures; and they were so arranged that men could pass from one room to another without perceiving any inequality (in the floor)."

The Mahābhārata contains short but comprehensive accounts of the cities of Dvārakā (III.15), Indraprastha (1.207, 30f), a floating city (III. 173, 3), Mithilā (III. 207, 7) and others.

In the Sabhā-parva there are interesting descriptions of some assembly-halls. Maya built an assembly-hall for the Pāṇḍavas (chapter I). A description is given also of the assembly-hall of Indra (chapter VII), of Yama (chapter VIII), of Varuṇa (chapter IX), of Kubera (chapter X), and of Brahman (chapter XI).

A large number of houses were needed for the accommodation of the kings invited to Indraprastha on the occasion of King Yudhiṣṭhira's royal feast, *Rājasūya,* and the poet describes the lodgings assigned to the guest: "O king, these and many other princes of the middle country (India proper) came to the great ceremonial, *Rājasūya,* of the sons of Pāṇḍu. By order of the virtuous monarch to them were assigned dwellings replete with refreshments of every kind, and having by them charming lakes and ranges of ornamental plants................ Those houses were lofty as the peaks of the Kailāśa mountain, most charming in appearance, and provided with excellent furniture. They were surrounded on all sides by well-built high walls of a white colour. The windows were protected by golden lattices and decorated with a profusion of jewellery. The stairs were easy of ascent ; the rooms were furnished with commodious seats, and clothing, and garlands ; and the whole was redolent with the perfume of the finest agallochum. The houses were white as the goose, bright as the moon, and looked most picturesque even from a distance of four miles. They were free from obstructions, provided with doors of uniform height, but of various quality, and inlaid with numerous metal ornaments, even as the peak of the Himālaya. The princes were refreshed by the very sight of those mansions."

"In the story of Nala, allusion is made to a lofty balcony from which men were seen from a great distance ; and in the Rāmāyaṇa, Mantharā........ looks out from an upper window of the palace to notice the rejoicings of the people in the street on the nomination of Rāma to the Vice-Kingship of Kośala.

"In the city [described in the epics] special palaces existed for the King, the princes, the chief priests, ministers, and military officers. Besides these and humble dwellings (the larger houses being divided into various courts), there were various assembly-halls, courts of justice, and the booths of small traders with goldsmith's shops, and the work-places of other artisans."

"The words *toraṇa,* arched gateway ; *harmya,* masonry house ; *devāyatana,* temple ; *sabhā,* assembly-hall ; *prāsāda,* palace ; *śikhara,* steeple ; and *vimāna,* pavilion, in the above extract [from the Rāmāyaṇa] are noteworthy. None of them can consistently be applied to huts and thatched houses for which the poets invariably use different words. Prurient fancy may extol and exaggerate, but it never suffices to create names of material objects which the fanciful have never seen or heard of ; a Ruskin may amuse himself and his readers by building an imaginary palace in the air, but his ideas are always of the earth, earthly, taken from material objects with which he is familiar.

The Puranas

The Purāṇas generally deal with the subject of architecture in more detail than the classes of literature referred to above. Casual references like those given above from the preceding classes of literature are frequently met with in all the nineteen great Purāṇas. Some nine Purāṇas have, however, treated the subject more systematically, and have materially contributed to the later *Śilpa-śāstras* themselves. *The Matsya-Purāṇa,* for instance, has eight comprehensive chapters dealing in great detail with architecture and sculpture. In one of these chapters accounts are given of eighteen ancient architects. One chapter is devoted to the column which is the regulator of the whole composition of a building. Columns are divided into five classes, as in the western system, and their component parts into eight mouldings exactly like those of the Graeco-Roman orders. Buildings are described in two chapters together with their architectural details, such as plans, measures, classifications, pavilions, halls, storeys, steeples, and cupolas. Some of the building materials are also discussed in a separate chapter. The remaining three chapters are devoted exclusively to sculpture. One of these deals with a very technical subject, namely, the *tālamāna* or proportionate measures of an image ; and in the other two the images of the Phallus and its Pedestal are described.

The *Skanda,* which is another early Purāṇa, has devoted three chapters to the subject. One of these refers to the laying out of a large city. In another, mention is made of the construction of a golden hall and three chariots in accordance with the descriptions supplied, and the names of the architects are added. The details of the construction of a special pavilion for the wedding of a royal princess is described in another chapter wherein reference is made to the painting also. Sculpture is associated with architecture ; but painting is hardly mentioned in these works.

The *Garuḍa-purāṇa* makes some valuable additions to the contributions of this class of literature to architecture. One of the four chapters devoted to this subject deals systematically with all the three classes of buildings, namely, residential, military and religious, as well as with the laying out of pleasure-gardens and pavilions therein. Thus, in this chapter residential buildings, forts and fortified towns, temples and monasteries are described along with garden-houses. The following chapter treats exclusively of religious buildings. The remaining two chapters are devoted to sculpture, one dealing with rules regarding the construction of an image and the other with the installation of images in temples.

The *Agni,* among all the Purāṇas, has dilated on the subject at great length. There are sixteen chapters of which one deals with town-planning, two with residential buildings and the remaining thirteen with sculpture. The importance of its contributions to the *Śilpa-śāstra* lies, however, specially in two things. First, it seems to have been aware of the *Mānasāra,* the standard work on architecture. Secondly, its chapter on town-planning is a real addition to the Purāṇas' contributions to architecture. Temples and residential buildings are described in two chapters. The treatment of sculpture also is unique, and is the most exhaustive of all the accounts given in the Purāṇas. It deals with almost all the classes of religious images, both of male and female deities, as well as of those not falling under either of these categories. Thus, of the thirteen chapters on sculpture, one is devoted to the description of the sun-god, one to the ten incarnations of Viṣṇu, two others also to Viṣṇu under the name of Vāsudeva, one to the guardian angel of the house, one to the goddess of fortune, two to the female deities in general, four to the Phallus and its Pedestal, and the remaining one to the stone gods, Śālagrāma and others.

The *Nārada-purāṇa* practically completes the Purāṇas' contributions to architecture. In a single chapter it describes the construction of pools, wells and tanks as well as temples. The *Linga-purāṇa* supplements the contributions by adding an account of the construction of sacrificial pits togethr with a description of temples and the installation of deities therein.

The *Vāyu,* which is one of the very early Purāṇas, maintains its unique position by dealing with the construction of various temples built upon mountain tops. Examples of these temples are still found on several peaks of the Himālaya and the Vindhya ranges. For the *Brahmāṇḍa-purāṇa* there was very little left to add. In a single chapter it describes the construction of temples and residential buildings.

The *Bhaviṣya,* apparently a late Purāṇa, has also nothing new to contribute. Three of its chapters are devoted to sculpture. Architecture proper, comprising the description of temples is treated in a single chapter. The most striking featrue of this Purāṇa is that the number, name and other architectural details of the buildings described in it are identical with the twenty types found in the *Matsya-purāṇa,* and the *Bṛhat-saṁhitā* of Varāhamihira.

The *Bṛhat-saṁhitā,* usually classed under the astronomical and astrological treatises, is but a semi-Purāṇa, dealing, as it does, with heterogeneous subjects like the Purāṇas themselves. Its authorship is attributed to Varāhamihira who is supposed to be one of the nine traditional gems in the court of a mythical Vikramāditya, and is thus imagined to be a contemporary of Kālidāsa a poet of unrivalled fame. In this treatise there are but five chapters devoted to both architecture and sculpture. But the subjects have been treated with a master hand. The chapters open with a definition of the science of architecture, and the author goes on to describe, briefly but succinctly and to the point, the suitable building sites, testing of soil, general plan, comparative measures of storeys and doors, and carvings thereon, and other important parts of a building.

The preliminary subjects are described in the opening chapter. Then follows the description of the buildings proper under the same twenty types as in the *Matsya* and *Bhaviṣya-purāṇas,* the names and details being identical. The preparation of cement is discussed in a separate chapter. One whole chapter is devoted to the construction of the necessary articles of house-furniture, such as bedsteads, couches, and seats. Quite consistently with his sense of proportion Varāhamihira devotes only one chapter to sculpture, where too the details of images are described in a scientific manner which is distinctly missing in other ancient literature. He is however, accused of being "in the habit of uncritically copying his authorities and misappropriating their materials. But in his treatise seven architecture authorities are mentioned distinctly.

The Agamas

The *Āgamas,* like the *Purāṇas,* incidentally deal with architectural subjects ; their contributions to the *Śilpa-śāstra* are, however, more extensive and valuable. Some of the *Āgamas* deal with very technical matters, which are not me with in the *Purāṇas.* Moreover, some *Āgamas* to all intents and purposes are but architectural treatises. The *Kāmikāgama,* for instance, devotes sixty chapters out of a total of seventy-five to architecture and sculpture, and its treatment of the subjects can hardly be surpassed by that of an avowedly architectural treatise. Just like a *Śilpa-śāstra* it begins systematically with the preliminary matters, such as the testing and preparation of soil, selection of sites, scheme of measurement and the finding out of the cardinal points by means of gnomons for the orientation of buildings, and the ground plans. Buildings proper are described under twenty types, just as in the *Matsya* and *Bhaviṣya-purāṇas,* as well as the *Bṛhat-saṁhitā.* But, unlike the *Purāṇas,* there is in the *Kāmikāgama* a discussion of architectural matters under some very highly technical classifications, such as the styles, Nāgara, Drāviḍa and Vesara ; shapes, masculine, feminine, and neuter ; Śuddha, Miśra, and Saṁkīrṇa, depending respectively on a single material, mixture of two materials, and the amalgamation of many materials ; Saṁcita, Asaṁcita and Apasaṁcita otherwise known as Sthānaka, Āsana, and Śayana, which, in case of temples, depend on the erect sitting, and reclining postures of the image. Another very technical matter referred to is *āyādi* formulas so very important in selecting the right proportions.

The *Karaṇāgama* also devotes much space to architecture and sculpture. There are thirty-seven chapters in this *Āgama,* which deal with these subjects exhaustively. It makes a distinct addition to the *Āgamas'* contributions to the *Śilpa-śāstras.* It contributes two valuable chapters dealing with the details of the nine and *ten-tāla* measures. This is also a highly technical matter concerning sculpture and entirely missing in the *Purāṇas* also has close similarities with the *Mānasāra.*

The *Suprabhedāgama* has devoted only fifteen chapters to architecture and sculpture. Nor has it any thing new to add to the *Āgamas'* contributions to the *Śilpa-śāstras.* But its unique nature consists in the fact that it has quite successfully summarised all important matters in a comparatively small space, and in respect of brevity, explicitness and precision it surpasses even the *Bṛhat-saṁhitā* of Varāhamihira. This *Āgama* has apparently drawn upon a *Śilpa-śāstra.* Its similarities with the *Mānasāra,* discussed elsewhere in detail.

The *Vaikhānosāgama* has two chapters on sculpture, one of which deals with the general description of images and the other with the *ten-tāla* measures. The *Aṁśumad-bhedāgama* has a single chapter on the *ten-tāla* measures. Instances like those given above can be culled from the remaining *Āgamas* also, but the multiplication of illustrations is not likely to furnish any new information. It is, however, clear that architecture was a favourite subject for the authors of the *Āgamas* also.

Miscellaneous Treatises

The works on royal polity deal with architectural matters in a more than casual way. The Kauṭilīya *Arthaśāstra,* for instance, devotes some seven chapters to the subject, containing a large number of structural details. There are interesting descriptions of forts, fortified cities, town-planning, and military and residential buildings.

The *Śukra-nīti* deals with both architectural and sculptural objects. Rules and structural details are given along with interesting descriptions of forts and fortified towns, of temples and other kinds of buildings, and of various sorts of images. In this treatise sculptural details are more numerous in some respects than even in the *Śilpa-śāstras.* Repair of broken images, for instance, is an important matter in sculpture, which has been dealt with in detail in this treatise. Another important contribution made by the *Śukra-nīti* to the *Śilpa-śāstras* is the description of the *seven-tāla* measures which are generally applicable, both in India and the West, to well proportioned human figures only.

Avowedly historical works are not numerous in Saṁskṛt. Of the two treatises, one is concerned with the reign of a single king and the other with the events of a country covering many reigns. In both these treatises architecture has been given its already well-recognized place.

The *Harṣa-carita* is a history of Harṣavardhana of Kanauj, during whose reign the famous Chinese traveller Hieun Tsang visited India. In this history it is stated that "the palace had besides the harem always more than three courtyards ; the outer one being for people and for state reception, the next inner one for *Śardārs* (chiefs or nobles) and the third one for intimate persons only. The palaces were stately buildings, though not of stone. The floors, however, are described as made of shining stones. The columns and walls were ornamented with gold and even precious stones. There was usually a several storeyed building with inner gardens of flower-beds and large fruit trees." Mention is made also of detached buildings like the *Maṇḍapas* or pavilions for the purposes of *sabhā* (council-hall), *satra* (inn), *prapā* (drinking-house) and *prāg-vaṁśa.* The useful articles of house furniture, such as thrones (*siṁhāsana*), couches (*śayana*), and *āsandi,* meaning chairs, are also described.

The *Rājataraṅgiṇī* of Kalhaṇa, dealing with the history of Kashmir, refers frequently to architectural objects like castles (*Bāna-śālā*), monumental buildings (*Caitya*) and monasteries (*Vihāras*). But in these references very few structural details are to be met with. The references of Kalhaṇa to temples and other buildings also generally lack constructive details. But interesting structural details of some shrines merely referred to in Kalhaṇa's work are elaborated by Major C.B. Bates in the Gazetteer of Kashmir and have been given in a note by Sir M. A. Stein.

The astrological and astronomical treatises frequently refer to architectural topics, especially those bearing upon auspicious times. In a pamphlet of this class twenty-one things are stated to be observed in connection with building a house. A famous astronomical treatise, the *Gārga-saṁhitā,* deals with a large number of purely architectural subjects, such as the courts, compounds, compartments, rooms, dimensions, and location of doors.

The more authoritative works like the *Sūrya-siddhānta,* the *Śiddhāntaśiromaṇi,* and the *Līlāvatī* deal exhaustively with a very technical matter bearing upon architecture, namely, the description of gnomons which were used for finding out cardinal points. The subject is architecturally very important, inasmuch as it refers to the orientation of buildings.

The poetical works of Kālīdāsa, Bhavabhūti and others refer occasionally to architectural matters. In the *Vikramorvaśī,* for instance, mention is made of a flight of stairs made like the waves of the Ganges. The *Uttara-Rāma-Carita* refers to an architecturally important matter, namely, cement which is specially described in some *Śilpa-śāstras.* In the same work Nala, the son of the heavenly architect Viśvakarman, is mentioned as an engineer who built the bridge joining India with Ceylon.

Of this class of works, the *Mṛcchakaṭika* which is a modernized drama, dealing as it does with the ordinary affairs of worldly people, refers very frequently to architectural matters which are too numerous to be included here. A very interesting description of the gateway and as many as eight courtyards into which the whole compound is divided, is given in the fourth Act. This description is further full of architectural details. This reference is specially important owing to the fact that in the *Mānasāra* as well as the *Purāṇas* and the *Āgamas* the compound, however big it may be, is divided into not more than five courts, the fourth of which is technically called *prākāra* in the *Mānasāra.*

Traces of an advanced state of architecture are found also in works like grammars and lexicons. Yāska in his *Nirukta* mentions several words which can be used for masonry houses only. In the later lexicons like the *Amarakośa* lists of several architectural terms are met with. Derivations of words like *bhāṣkara,* sculptor ; *iṣṭaka,* brick ; *stambha,* pillar ; *aṭṭālikā,* edifices are found in Pāṇini's grammar. They no doubt imply the existence of brick and stone buildings in those times.

CHAPTER 1

IDEAL HOME PLANNING

Selection of Site

There are sixteen types of land formations. They can be broadly grouped under three categories. They are: forest lands, fertile lands, and ordinary lands.

Type of Land

A land that is fertile, verdant, has hills and valleys around, has tall and sweet scented trees and shrubs, where the atmosphere is serene, cool, and calm, where songs of birds abound, such a location is ideal for the selection of a dwelling site.

Type of Soil

The ground should have sweet, dense, soft, and pleasant soil. It should be quadrangular, must have south to west high, slopes towards north or east or northeast

It should have a pond on the southern side*. Free from vermin, ants, rats, shells, bones, skulls, and holes. The soil should be clayey, scratchy, the crusty, without husks, ashes, and gravels.

Ground to be Avoided

Soil having the smell of honey, ghee (clarified butter), having burnt smell, smell of birds, fish or rotten body, adjacent to royal palaces, tomb, road crossings, having thorny trees, uneven, circular, triangular, concave, rounded, adjacent to workshop and factories, infested with poisonous snakes, frequented by monkeys, bears, foxes, abode of owls, lions, cats, and other wild animals, having

*As per Mānasāra.

thorny trees should be avoided. Similarly a ground having access from all around should be avoided.

Suitable Ground

Ground having various colours, taste, fertile, redolent like musk by black bees, having all good features, such a land should be selected and purified for building.

Examination of Soil

The selected ground should be examined as described below:

First the master of the house to be built should find out an auspicious moment as specified in the Jyotiṣśāstra. On the day selected, he should take bath in the morning, fast, keep a calm and steady mind. At the chosen auspicious moment, he should put on garland of white flowers, then should offer obeisance to the deities with milk and sugar. After that he should prepare a pit on the ground. The pit should be precisely quadrangular and one cubit (63.65 cm) deep. It should be filled with water to the brim. Next day morning after bath he should sit facing east with a steady mind, then should offer prayer to mother earth for blessing in the undertaking. The next day he along with the sthāpati should examine the water in the pit. If some water is left in the soil it is taken to be good. If it is dried up or still wet it denotes the loss of wealth and destruction. If the cavity is filled with the same earth dugout from that pit, the soil is fair, if it is not filled up it is bad. If it is over filled the soil is good. After the test the master should go round the ground and make sure that all parts are equally good. The ground thus chosen should be all productive in order to secure all prosperity.

Erection of Gnomon and Pegs*

On the day before the fixing of the gnomon the area should be purified, levelled accurately after watering. In the middle of selected spot a quadrangular of four cubic (2.46 m) should be made.

The fixing of the gnomon and pegs should be done in the early

*Drawings are given at the end.

morning on an auspicious day, excepting the full or new moon day. After fixing the gnomon should be left for the whole day. The wood suitable for making a gnomon are: Cassia fistula, Sami, Sandal wood, Redsanders, Acacia catechu, ebony, minsops kanki, white milk tree, or subha daṇḍa (tooth tree).

There are three types of gnomon. They are: the long, middle, and the short type.

Long Type

It has a length of one cubic or 24 angulas or 18″ (63.65 cm). Its width at the bottom is 6 angulas or 4.5″ or 17.55 cm. The width at the top being 2 angulas or 1.5″ or 5.85 cm.

Middle Type

It has a length of 18 angulas or 13.5″ or 52.65 cm. Its bottom width being 5 angulas or 14.65 cm. and the top width being 2.95 cm.

Smaller Type

The smaller type of gnomon will have a length of twelve angulas or 35.10 cm. The width being four angulas or 11.70 cm. at the bottom and the top having 3/4 angulas or 1.65 cm. Yet another type of gnomon can also be made having a length of 9 angulas and the width at the bottom and top calculated accordingly.

Ascertaining the correct Eastwest Direction

At the centre of the prepared site a circle having a radius double that of the selected gnomon should be drawn using a chord. The gnomon should be firmly fixed at the centre of the circle. At a fixed time in a forenoon the shadow from the gnomon touching the circumference of the circle on the west should be marked. Similarly in the afternoon shadow from the gnomon touching the circumference should be marked in the east.

To find the northsouth direction bisect the eastwest line with east and west points as centres and diameter as radius. Join the cutting points through the centre. Again divide the 45 degree formed at the centre to obtain northeast, southeast, southwest, northwest points. Draw parallel perpendicular to northsouth line from east and west points to obtain the northwest, northeast, southeast, and southwest points.

In finding out the correct eastwest direction it is necessary to take into consideration the Apa-chchhāyā (light shadow) for every ten days in each month of the year. The table given explains it. It gives the number of angulas to be left out in each month.

(Apa-chchhāyā to be left out in angulas)

Months	*1st 10 days*	*Middle 10 days*	*Last 10 days*
Makara (Dec/Jan)	8 angulas	7 angulas	6 angulas
Kumbha (Jan/Feb)	6 angulas	5 angulas	4 angulas
Meena (Feb/Mar)	4 angulas	3 angulas	2 angulas
Mesha (Mar/Apr)	2 angulas	1 angulas	Nil.
Vṛiṣha (Apr/May)	Nil	1 angulas	2 angulas
Mithuna (May/June)	2 angulas	3 angulas	4 angulas
Kulina (June/July)	4 angulas	3 angulas	2 angulas
Siṁha (July/Aug)	2 angulas	1 angulas	Nil.
Kanyā (Aug/Sep)	Nil	1 angulas	2 angulas
Tulā (Sep/Oct)	2 angulas	3 angulas	4 angulas
Vṛiśchika (Oct/Nov)	4 angulas	5 angulas	6 angulas
Dhanu (Nov/Dec)	6 angulas	7 angulas	8 angulas

During these months solar zodiac happens to be a constellation during the last twenty days. During this period the apa-chchhāyā should be taken as nil. In these solar months even if those constellations take place only occasionally apa-chchhāyā should be left out. It has been so discredited by ancient sages to accept or reject in case of doubt to the extent of ten angulas.

Accordingly the architect should use the chord to find out cardinal points. As per the data given above the eastwest line should be determined exactly.

Suitable directions for the construction of building and temples are:

Northeast direction is best for residential buildings.
East is suited for temples.

Southeast brings evil.

Making the Plots

Thirtytwo ground plans are given in Mānasāra. They are for buildings, villages, towns, palaces, forts etc. They are:

1. The first one is a site of one plot, which may be square, rectangular, round, oval or sixteen sided, it is called Sakala;

2. the second is of four plots named Paiśācha or Pechaka;
3. the third, Pīṭha, is of 9 plots;
4. the fourth, Mahāpīṭha, is of 16 plots;
5. the fifth Upapīṭha, is of 25 plots;
6. the sixth, Ugra-pīṭha, is of 16 plots;
7. the seventh, Sthaṇḍila, is of 49 plots;
8. the eighth, Chhandita, is to 64 plots;
9. the ninth, Parama-sayika, is of 81 plots;
10. the tenth, Asana, is of 100 plots;
11. the eleventh, Sthaniya, is of 121 plots;
12. the twelfth, Deśya, is of 144 plots;
13. the thirteenth, Ubhayachandita, is of 169 plots;
14. the fourteenth, Bhadra, is of 196 plots;
15. the fifteenth, Mahāsana, is of 225 plots;
16. the sixteenth, Padma-garbha, is the 256 plots;
17. the seventeenth, Triyuta, is of 289 plots;
18. the eighteenth, Karashtaka, is of 324 plots;
19. the nineteenth, Ganita, is of 369 plots;
20. the twentieth, Suryavisalaka, is of 400 plots;
21. the twenty-first, Susaṁhītā, is of 441 plots;
22. the twenty-second, Supratikānta, is of 484 plots;
23. the twenty-third, Visalaka, is of 529 plots;
24. the twenty-fourth, Vipula-bhoga, is of 576 plots;
25. the twenty-fifth, Viveśa, is of 625 plots;
26. the twenty-sixth, Vipula-bhoga, is of 676 plots;
27. the twenty-seventh, Viprakānta, is of 729 plots;
28. the twenty-eight, Visalaksha, is of 784 plots;
29. the twenty-ninth, Vipra-bhakti, is of 841 plots;
30. the thirtieth, Visvesa-sara, is of 900 plots;
31. the thirty-first, Īśvarakānta, is of 961 plots; and
32. the thirty-second, Chandrakānta, is of 1,024 plots.

Dwelling Houses

Five types of dimensions are given that are suitable for the setting up of dwelling houses. They are:

1. The length of the house should be equal or greater than the breadth by one-fourth, or one half or three-fourth or twice.
2. The length may be greater than twice by one-fourth, one half three-fourth or three times.

3. The length may be greater than three times by one one-fourth, one-half, three-fourth or four times.

Thus the proportion between the length and breadth of the house has to be determined.

The Parama-sayika plan of 81 plots is the most ideal for a dwelling house. The length and breadth should be marked for this plan as per anyone of the five given dimensions (breadth and length). The minimum being two and three daṇdas (2.56 m). That is the minimum breadth 5.90 m and the length 7.638 m. The maximum being ten and eleven daṇḍas or breadth 25.60 m and the length 28.16 m, the increment being by 5.12 meters proportionally. See for details of each plot in the plan drawing for eighty-one plots at the end.

In this the centre nine plots are known as Brahma.

Eight plots outside this is Daivaka, 16 plots beyond this Manusha and the 24 plots outside are known as Piśācha.

Plot Allotment

The middle nine plots are assigned to Brahma. This area is to be left open.

The Arya, Vivasvat, Mitra and Bhudhara are suited for Brahmins, Kṣhatriyas and Vaiśyas. Similarly the four quarters namely, the east (Indra), etc. are suitable for the dwelling of the twice-born. The plots known as Daivaka (of gods), beginning from Āpavatsa are suitable for the other castes.

The Yama and the Varuṇa plots in the south and west respectively are suitable for the main houses of the Kṣhatriyas (kings).

The Varuṇa and the Soma plots in the west and north respectively are suitable for the residence of the Vaiśyas (Merchant class).

The southwest, north, and the northeast plots are suitable for the houses of the Śūdras.

The northwest and the southeast quarters are suitable for the residences of all.

Water bodies should be made in northeast side.[1] South or southwest is suitable for the dining hall for all people. Satyaka or the Antariksha plots are suited for the bedroom for all. The rooms

1. In *Vishwakarma Prakash,* wells and others water bodies i.e. ponds, wells etc. should be in northeast corner.

for enjoyment (entertainment) should be located in the Sosha, Asura, or Varuṇa plots. In the north, northeast or in the Parjanya plot should be the kitchen for all.[2] But as per "Viswakarma Prakasha" kitchen should be in southeast corner. Aditi plot is suited for bathroom for all.

In the Indra or the Indrarāja plots should be located the dressing room.

Study room should be in the Mṛiga plot.

Treasury (strong room) for keeping valuables should be located in the Soma and Mṛiga plots.

For servants quarters Indra and Mahendra plot is suitable.

Boys room should be in the Savitra plot.

Girls apartments should be Rudrajaya plot.

The room for amusement and luxuries should be built in the Soma plot. Family chapel should be located in the Nāga plot. Store room should be built either in the Nāga or Mukhyaka plot.

The flower Pavillion (garden) should be located in Sosha, or Asura plot.

The main doors of the houses of all people should be either in the Mahendra, Pushpadanta, Mukhya or Grihakshata plot. The temple for all people may be built in the Mukhya plot. Near the Brahma plot (central area), the pavilion for wedding and other ceremonies should be built. Steps are to be put up at the four corners and four directions.

The measurement of the wall of all houses should be made in proportion to the measurement of the court. At the gate, there should be gate house.

---

2. In *Vishwakarma Prakash,* southeast corner is suitable for kitchen.

CHAPTER 2

IDEAL VILLAGE PLANNING

Villages

According to shape, the villages have been divided into eight types or classes. They are:

1. Daṇḍaka
2. Sarvotabhadra
3. Nandyāvarta
4. Padmaka
5. Svastika
6. Prastara
7. Kārmuka
8. Chaturmukha.

The General Plan of a Village

Each village is surrounded by a wall made of brick or stone, strong and high enough to prevent leaping over. Beyond this wall there is a ditch broad and deep enough to cause an obstruction in the event of an attack on the village. There are generally four main gates at the middle of the four sides and as many at the four corners. Inside the wall there is a large street round the village. This street is generally used for circumambulation on some special occasion, daily round of the police, open-air drive etc. Two other large streets are those which run from one gate to another in the middle of the wall on each side. They intersect each other at the centre of the village, where a temple or a hall is generally built for village assembly. The village is thus divided into four main blocks, each of which is again sub-divided into many blocks by streets which are always straight from one end to the other of a main block. The ground floor of the houses on the main streets are used as shops. The surrounding street has footpaths and houses only on one side. These houses are mainly public buildings, such as schools, colleges, libraries, guest houses etc. All other streets generally have residential buildings on both side. The houses of high or low are always uniform in make. Congestion is carefully avoided. The drains are made towards the slope of the village. Tanks and ponds are provided in all the inhabited areas and located in such places as can be conveniently reached by the people with ease. The temples of public worship as well public gardens and parks are similarly located. The people of the same caste or vocation are generally housed in the same areas.

The experience of many generations have proved that the plan of villages were best for purposes of defence, and healthy living. The easterly axis of the plan ensured that the principal streets receive abundant sun rays throughout the day; while the intersection of main streets being shorter ones running north and south provide a perfect circulation of air and the utmost benefit of the cool breezes. The *Mānasāra* recognizes forty different types of villages and towns according to the extent of the land owned by them; commencing with a village-unit which is 500 daṇḍas.

The *Mānasāra* gives the maximum width of the main street of a village as 5 daṇḍas (a daṇḍa – 8 feet). The other varied in width from 1 to 5 daṇḍas. The size of a small house was reckoned as being 24 feet or by 16 to 40 feet by 32 feet. They were generally grouped together by four, so as to form an inner square or quadrangle. The magic of the square afforded the best protection of the house-hold. (The scale used for measuring land is a bit different from the one prescribed for measuring a dwelling. For dwelling it is 24 angulas or 2.56 m whereas for land it is 27 angulas or 2.786 m.)

Planning a Village

The land site selected for a village should be measured first. Next the ground plan should be marked. After that sacrificial offering should be made. Next the village-planning should be done. This should be followed by planning of residential and other buildings. Laying the foundations of buildings. Finally the first entry into the houses should be considered.

For village planning the unit of measurement used is rod termed as Dhanurgraha of 27 angulas.

Another vital matter to be considered is the auspicious measure under āya rules according to Jyotiṣśāstra. It is known as Shadvarga. It is given as under:

Āya the remainder of	L x 8/12
Vyaya the remainder of	B x 9/10
Rikṣha (Nakṣhatra or group of stars of 27)	L x 8/27
Yoni (The eight directions)	B x 3/8
Vāra (7 week days)	C x 9/7 or T x 9/7 or Hx 9/7
Tithi Aṁśa (according to moon cycle)	C x9/30
Aṁśa	Cx4/9

(L—Length, B—Breadth, C—Circumference, T—Thickness, H—Height).

Gaṇa: All gaṇas except Asura and Manusha are good.

Nayana: To ascertain the Nayana the total days from Sunday to Saturday (seven days) is multiplied by three to which is added the Aśvinī or any other nakṣhatra of the day and whole is divided by the total days. Number six is first Nayana, 7th second, 8th third, 9th and so on.

The names of the different classes of formulas, such as Āya, Vyaya, Vāra, etc. represent well-known group of objects that always follow a certain serial order. Āya represents the group of twelve beginning with Sidhi. Vyaya represents the group of ten beginning with Śikhara. Rikṣha represents the well known group of twenty-seven planets. Yoni represents the group of eight symbols namely Dhwaja, Dhuma, Siṁha, Swā, Vṛisha, Khara, Kunjara, and Kāka. Vāra represents the group of seven days in a week, Tithi represents the group of thirty lunar days comprising fourteen of the dark half, fourteen of the light half, new moon day and full moon day. And Aṃśa represents the group of nine beginning with Taskara.

It should be noticed that the measurement of length is tested by the formulas under Āya and Rikṣha, or breadth under Vyaya and Yoni and of circumference or height, under Vāra and Tithi.

It will be noted that the formula in each case consists of the product of the measurement to be considered and a certain other number divided by a figure which corresponds to the number constituting the group or series under which it is placed.

In each case, therefore, by resolving the formula, the remainder that may be left can be referred to that particular number in the series represents by that class, and if this happens to be one that under the conditions prevailing would be considered auspicious then the particular measurement would be acceptable, if not it would have to be rejected. For example if in a particular instance b x 3/8 coming under the class Yoni, the remainder left is two, it will point to the second Yoni Dhuma. If this Yoni is stated to be inauspicious, then the particular measurement of breadth cannot be approved. If again in the formula for Vāra, cx 9/7 the remainder happens to be 4, it will indicate the 4th day (Wednesday) of the week, and if it be stated to be auspicious, the circumference selected satisfies the test. The auspicious and inauspicious remainders.

When there is no remainder left in the formula of 'Āya' it increases religious merit, and when there is no remainder left in the formula of "Vyaya" it is auspicious. There is no defect if the 'Āya' be equal to "Vyaya".

Besides what has been said before regarding Āya and Vyaya the following too has to be noticed. In the calculation of Vāra if the remainder shows Friday, Monday, or Wednesday it is auspicious. However the bad effects of a day do not harm if there happens to be an auspicious yoga or conjunction of planets. If on any of the four days commencing from Sunday there happens to be the conjunction or Gaṇa of the stars starting with Viśākhā and ending at Svātī, they are respectively known as *Ganda-yoga, Mṛityu* (death) Yoga and *Sidhi* (success) Yoga. As regards Tithis of the new moon days, Aṣṭamī (eighth day) after the new or full moon and Navamī (ninth day) should be avoided. Rest of the Tithies are auspicious. As regards Rāsi leaving aside Vṛiśchika all other Rāsi's are auspicious.

Different Types of Villages*

There are eight kinds of villages. These are:

1. Daṇḍaka
2. Sarvatobhadra
3. Nandyāvarta

*. Illustrations are given at the end.

4. Padmaka
5. Svastika
6. Prastara
7. Kārmuka
8. Chaturmukha

Each of these has further sub-divisions according to different dimensions.

1. Daṇḍaka Village

It is the smallest type of village. It is suited for retired life. It is fit for the residence of Brahmins. In this village there may be houses ranging from twelve to three hundred, or there may be twelve houses of anchorites ('maunin', i.e. those who take the vow of silence). If it is meant for a hermitage it should be situated in a forest valley or on top of a hill. Depending on the type of people staying in the village or the place it is located its nomenclature differs. If it is an abode of hermits it is known as *Grāma* (village), if it is at the bank of a river it is known as *Pura,* if it has an assemblage of fifty initiated Brahmins known as Dikṣhitas it is called Nagar (Town). When there is a group of fifty to eighty Brahmins households it is known as *Maṅgala;* if the number of Brahmin household is one hundred it is called a *Koṣṭha* (see plate for details of layout at the end).

2. Sarvatobhadra Village

One hundred and fifty-seven kinds of designs are given, starting from sixty-one rod, breadth to three hundred and thirteen rods. This has two types. One is known as Maṇḍūka and the other Sthaṇḍila. Its shape is square (see plate for details of layout at the end). In the centre of the village, there should be temple for Brahmā, Viṣṇu, or Śiva. It can be the residence of hermits known as Tapasvin, Yati, Brahmachāriṇ, Yogin, Buddhist, Jains, or of house-holders. For security, the village should have surrounding wall and a ditch around it. At the four directions there should be main gates, as well as smaller gates. It should have one or two or three, four or five carriage roads together with the surrounding street. Among the roads the internal ones should have one footpath and the outer one two footpaths. In the Paiśācha part there should be a smaller street running through all the plots. The temple for the guardian deity should be on the out side of the Paiśācha part towards the northeast direction. The street in this area should be frog shaped (Nandyavarta). This street should have footpaths on both sides. At the four corner within namely the northwest, south-west, northeast should be built monastery, temple and guest house respectively and at the southeast the drinking house. The public buildings can be built in any quarter as desired. At the four corners at the end of the internal carriage roads there should be a maṭh (cloister) for a guru (preacher).

The locations of the houses of people of various professions are:

All kinds of workmen or labourers should be on the high way. The houses of Vaiśyas and Śūdras in the southern side. Milkmen quarters between east and southeast. Beyond these should be the cowsheds.

The houses of the weavers should be located between the south and the west. Beyond this should be the houses of tailors, leather workers etc.

The blacksmiths residences should be between west and northwest. Beyond this should be the houses of the fish mongers and butchers.

Between north and the northwest should be residences of clerical community, therein also should be houses of Physicians (Vaidyas) rather of the medical caste (Ambasthas) etc.

On the outskirts of the wall should be homes of people who deal in the bark of tress (especially tanners), and oil men.

At some distance from the village in the northern outskirts should be the temple for Vaiśṇavī and Chāmūṇḍā. Beyond this should be houses for those who take care of the crematories. In the south, west or southwest should be the village tanks for bathing and for drinking water.

3. Nandyāvarta Village

The length and breadth of this type of village can be equal or the length may be greater. There are two hundred and five kinds in this type of village. The minimum size starts with a breadth of one hundred and fifty seven rods and ends at five hundred and sixty five rods, the increment being by two rods. This village is said to be good for the residence of Brahmins. If the length and breadth of the village are equal the ground plan adapted is Chandita or Maṇḍuka (sixty-four plots). If the length is greater than the breadth the Paramasayika (eighty-one plots) plan is used. If the length and breadth are equal the Sthaṇḍila (fortynine plots) is used. The broad distribution of the Chandita design is as follows:

> The four central plots is known as Brahma. The twelve plots, surrounding it, is known as Daivaka. The next twenty surrounding plots are known as Manusha; the next twenty-eight surrounding plots are known as Paiśācha. Total sixty-four plots.
> In the Parama-sayika design, the nine plots at the centre is known as Brahma; the next sixteen surrounding plots area is called Daivaka; and the next twenty-four surrounding plot areas is termed Manusha; and the final round of thirty-two plots area is known as Paiśācha. Total eighty-one plots.
> In the Sthaṇḍila plan the one plot at the centre is known as Brahma; the eight plots surrounding it is known as Daivaka; and the next sixteen surrounding plots are Manusha; and the last twenty-four surrounding plots are called Paiśācha. Total forty-nine plots.

Layout of the Nandyāvarta (Frog shaped) Village

If it is the residence of Brahmins it is known as Maṅgala. If it is the abode of Kṣhatriyas, Vaiśyas, and others, it is known as Pura. When the people staying there are only Vaiśyas and Śūdras and others it is called an Agrahara.

When it is occupied by all types of people the residential areas of each should be as follows: Brahmin houses should be in the Manusha and Daivaka areas. The royal palace should occupy Daivaka, Manusha, and Paiśācha areas. The houses of Vaiśyas, Śūdras, and others are to be located in the Paiśācha area.

The village should have protection wall all around. On the external side of the wall all around there should be ditch. It should have fencing all around. There should be large gates at the middle of the four corners and four directions. They can either be circular or square according to the plan. The gates located in the four directions should be the same at the opposite ends. In case it is felt that only two gates are enough, then it should be done in the east and west only. However the gates at the four corners should remain. Besides the main gates, small intermediates doors are to be provided at the Nāga, Mṛga, Aditi, Udita, Parjanya, Antarikṣha, Puśān, Vitatha, Gandharva, Bhṛṅgarāja, Sugrīva or Asura parts. Similarly drain gates should be located in the Mukhya, Bhallata, Mṛga, Udita, Jayanta, Mahendra, Satyaka, or Mṛṣa parts.

Streets and Roads

The eastern carriage-road should run from east to west in Paiśācha area. The southern street should run from east to west. The western street from south to north and the northern streets should run from west to east. There should be large streets both lengthwise and breadthwise; there should be one, three, five or seven such streets. They should have two footpaths. In place of these large streets there may be constructed one, two, three, four, or five smaller exterior roads without footpath. One footpath should run from along the two internal streets running from south to north at the two internal streets running from east to west. The remaining two should have two footpaths each. A street should be provided with footpaths, while a road should be without it. Between the large streets and roads there should be lanes without any bend. The width of the streets can vary from three to twelve rods. All the streets can have the same width or that can be of different. The large road as well as all the streets should be made strong and firm with broken lime stones. The width of the large road should be equal to the width of a street of nine rods width. It is good to have the width of the middle street equal to the width of the large road. In the same manner the width of a lane should be equal to a street in the middle. However if necessary it can be shorter by one-eighth or three-fourth, or half of the street. The width of a large road should be equal to three-fourth of the width of all other streets. Similarly the width of a narrow lane should have half or three-fourth the width of large roads. However in the interior of the village it may be smaller by one-eighth, three-fourth or half.

Residential Areas for Different Castes

The Varuna, Mitra, Jayanta or Rudrajaya parts are suited for the royal palace. The same locality is suited for the Kṣhatriya or warrior class too. The clerical community should be allotted the southwest. The residences of Brahmins should be within Manusha and Daivaka parts. The Asura or Soma part is suited for the residences of chiefs, lords and ministers. The houses belonging to the priests should be located in the Puśhpadaṇta part. In the Dāuvarika and Sugrīva parts should be the homes for watch and ward or guards. The drummers are to occupy the gandharva or roga or Śosha parts and so also the musicians and dancers. Architects and artisans are to have the Vāyu part. The Nāga or Mukhya part for netra-ratnākara (jewellers). The north part is for the houses of armor makers. The physicians are to reside in the Aditi and Udita parts. Village watchmen are to occupy the northeast or Jayanta parts. The palanquin bearers are to have the Mahendra part. The guest houses are to locate in the Bhṛśa or the Antarikṣha parts. On the eastern street should be the houses of oilmen. On the west should be houses of the fish sellers, butchers and hunters. The washermen are to stay in northwest, the dancers in the south or east. North and northwest parts are meant for tailors.

Third round:

The houses of the blacksmiths in the south.
The houses of the basket makers in north or southeast.
The houses of the weapon makers in west or east.
The houses of the leather workers in north.

The next round of plots is for the use of other professions.

4. Padmaka Village

The village of this type should be planned either in the Chandita or Sthaṇḍila design layout of sixty-four or forty-nine plots respectively. The residential buildings should be built at the four corners of six plots each divided by an oblique line called 'sula'. It is essential to have a public hall and a temple in the above mentioned plot area. The village should have four to eight streets. There should not be any cross street in the middle. All the carriage roads in the exterior as well as surrounding ones should have footpaths. For rest of the details the same pattern described for Nandyāvarta village should be followed.

5. Swastika Village

Parama-sayika plan (Eighty-one plots)

The interior layout of this village should be in the form of the mythical *Swastika*. This type of village is specially meant for the residence of kings. It should have rampart at the lower part and wall at the upper part all around. It should have ditch around. Should have watch towers on the wall. That should be guarded by Yakṣhas, Rudra, Nata, and others. There should be eight gates opened at all points of the Swastika village in the four directions. Two being on each side. Mṛga, Antarikṣha, Bhṛṅg-rāja, Mṛṣa, Sosha, Roga, Aditi, and Udita parts should also be provided with small gates. All the big gates should be shaped like a plough and the smaller gates should be provided with two shutters. The village should be provided with number of streets such as, street running from east to west at the middle of the village; another street from south to north running across it. The centre crossing should be made strong and hard with lime stone. Other streets to be provided in the village are: streets from east to north to northeast, south to southwest to southeast, west, southwest to south, and north to northwest to west. All these streets are to be around the village. After this the surrounding street connecting the end of these four streets. Thus is made the Swastika-shaped street design. There should be two streets across the centre, two at the top and two at the bottoms connecting the four directions and the four corners. They should be provided with four entrances at the four directions and extending up to the aforesaid middle streets and ending by the four corners. A street is made running from east to west by the middle, from east to northeast to north and to the centre. Similarly streets are to be provided running from south to north by the middle of the two lines from the centre to the east and another from southeast to the south joining of which the southeast block is formed. Yet another similar street is to be made running east to west by the middle of the southwest block is from the centre to the south and then to the southwest ending in the west. Similar street is to be formed running from south to north block (by the middle of the northwest) from northwest and north ending by the centre. The number of these streets may vary as required. The streets should have two footpaths. However the middle one should not have the same as it is reserved for conveyances. The width of the footpath should get narrow towards the end. The outer surrounding streets should be provided with two footpaths. The outside of which should be covered (with wall and ditch). In the Paiśācha round (last round) as well as all around the village carriage roads should be provided.

Sthānīya Plan (One hundred and twenty-one plots)

It should be laid out as was described for the Swastika plan. The same should be followed in the Deśya, Ubhaya-chandita and Bhadra plans. In these the palaces of Parshasnika and other classes of kings should be built at the Arya and other plots in the four directions. But not anywhere and everywhere. In the Sthānīya plan the royal palace may be built at central part of the four cardinal points or intermediate points; they may also be built leaving out the Brahma plot, at the Mitra Vivasvat, or Arya plots. The palace may have as many storeys as desired. In the Deśya (twelfth of one hundred and forty-four plots), the royal palace should be built in the middle of the Varuṇa plot. This is known as Saṁgrama plan. In the Ubhaya-chandita or thirteenth plan having one hundred and sixty-nine plots the royal palace should be located at the middle of the soma (north) as also Indrajaya (southwest) plots when laid out in the Vijaya plan (i.e. last of the four plans, i.e. the fourteenth one, called Bhadra). The above suggestion is for Adhirāj a class of kings. For kings of Narendra order, the palaces should be built at the Vivasvat and Indra-jaya plots in the Agata (Deśya) plan. In the Ubhaya-chandita plan (saṁgrama plan) at the soma and Indrajaya plots. In the Vijaya (Bhādra) plan at the Arka or Indra or the Rudra-rāja plots. For the palaces of the Parashnika and other classes of kings in the plans such as the Sthānīya (Deśya, Ubhaya-chandita, and Bhādra) the plots to be used are Arya and other in the four directions only and not anywhere and everywhere.

Residential buildings

The residential buildings should be situated around the temples. In the residential quarters on one side of the central street there should be one footpath. In the outer streets two footpaths for the convenience of the pedestrians.

A temple outside the village can be built as one wish.

Temples

In a Swastika village, in a temple built for Śiva, only Pasupati Liṅga* should be installed in it. All other types of liṅgas should be installed outside the town. Viṣṇu and Brahmā Images should

---

*There are varieties of Liṅgas such as Śiva, Pashupati, Kālamukha, Mahāvrata, Vāma, Bhairava, Samakarana, Vardamāna, Sivanka, and Svastika.

be installed in the temples inside the interior of the village. However Pancharatna form of Viṣṇu temple should be outside the village wall. Similarly temples for dieties like Durgā, Gaṇeś, Buddha, Jina, Kārtikeya, and others should be built outside the Swastika village. The temple for Chāmūṇḍā should be facing north in the northeast beyond the village. It should also be situated at a distance from the village. For the army a pavilion should be built outside the village towards the east, west, or northwest.

6. Prastara Village

This type of village should have either a square or rectangular shape. It is fit for the residence of Kṣhatriyas or Vaiśyas. The village may be planned out according to Parama-sayika (eighty-one plots) or Chandita (sixty-four plots) or the Sthaṇḍila (forty-nine plots) or another plan as one desire.

The village should be protected with a surrounding wall and a ditch. It should have four or eight or twelve gates at the end of the large streets. A large street should be constructed in the Paiśācha part. It should have footpaths on both sides extending round the village. In the Pechaka (four plots) and Pīṭha (of nine plots), streets should be in continuation of the street built in the Paiśācha part. It should be connected by streets or similarly expanded. Mahāpīṭa (of twenty-five plots) block should be connected by streets. One street being constructed on the Pīṭha block there should not be any other street across the centre of the village. But there should be constructed two streets, one running from east and another from south to north as said before (in Paiśācha). In the Mahāpīṭa block there should be three streets each way in all directions. The width of the streets should range between seven, eight, nine, ten or eleven rods. The number of plots consisting the several blocks should be determined and they should be marked. The end of the street in them should extend up to the end of the blocks. There should be a circular road around the Paiśācha part. Extending from the side of the circular street, there should be five or seven streets running towards the east and north. There should be eight blocks. There should be one, two, three, or four smaller *zig-zag* cross roads. In case the four plots of Pechaka are to be connected by roads, the same are marked by nine crossings. Similarly if the nine plots of the Pīṭha are to be linked there should be sixteen crossings. The same way if the Mahāpīṭha plots are to be linked there should be twenty crossings. In the second round termed as Deva part, four plots of Pechaka should be marked for blocks and also nine plots in Pīṭha. The western part of each of these blocks should align to the shape of the Prastara village. The temples and palaces should be arranged as said in earlier examples. The houses of the Vaiśyas too should be as stated in earlier examples. The stalls for various merchandise should be lined on either sides of the large roads. Such roads should have footpaths connecting to the palace.

7. Kārmuka Village

This type of village can be square (with length and breadth equal) or rectangular having the length longer or greater. There are three varieties in this type of village. They are: Pattana, Kheṭaka, and Kharvaṭa. Pattana has a predominant population of Vaiśyas, whereas Kheṭaka that of Śūdras. Kharvaṭa has the predominance of Kṣhatriyas. The architect should plan and plot the village according to the size of the land. Kārmuka village is built on the bank of a river or near the seaside. There should be junctions at the head of the streets. The streets in every quarter i.e. street connecting west and north another between south and west according to suitability. On the outside, these streets should have a bow shape. There should be one or two or three or four or five pair of streets. Large carriage roads should be provided. They should have footpath on either side. The cross roads should have a single footpath. The village should be provided with many gates as desired. There may or may not be any rampart for protection.

Various deities should be installed as stated in earlier examples. The Viṣṇu and Śiva temples should be at the junction of two streets. If not they can be built where there is no street. The Viṣṇu temple should have its back turned towards the village as it is said to be auspicious. The rest of the things should be done as mentioned before for other villages.

8. Chaturmukha Village

This village can either be square or rectangular in its layout. It should possess all round boundary wall accordingly. From the centre (Brahma plot) of the village four streets should run in the four directions (east, west, north, and south). A large street should be made around the village and it should be provided with two footpaths. Four gates should be provided at the end of the four cross roads emerging from the centre. Similarly on each side there should be one gate. There should also be smaller gates as was mentioned in the case of previously mentioned villages.

In the large surrounding streets should be the houses for all castes. If the village is pre-dominated by Śūdras it is known as Alaya. If on the other hand Brahmins are more it is called Padma. If the Vaiśyas predominate then it is called Kolaka. As per certain norms the residences of the twice born (Brahman, Kṣhatriyas, and Vaiśyas) can be built in all the four parts of the village. However if the houses of the Brahmins are located in the southeast, then the residences of Kṣhatriyas (lit. kings) should be in the southwest. In the same way if the houses of the Vaiśyas are situated in the northwest then that of the Śūdras should be in the northeast. The last round known as Paiśācha (fourth round) should contain the dwellings of all workmen.

Temples dedicated to Viṣṇu, Śiva (Rudra), and other Gods should be built in the village as described earlier.

Layout of Villages

Residential houses should be located in the areas which are free from the congested streets full of traffic. If it is done it will cause destruction and ruin. Therefore a wise architect should keep this in mind while planning a village or town. In case of doubt, the tradition existing in a certain place should be followed. It is to be noted that in ancient villages the Gods were installed only during festivals and special occasions. This too was done in the open vacant space in the village. This fact should be kept in mind in planning a village or town. After a village or town has been planned or built, before the first settlement in the same, it is necessary to do proper religious rituals and honours to the Gods installed there. This is essential for the welfare of the people who are to reside there. This ritual is the responsibility of the Sthapati or the architect who planned the village. Similarly if there is any ancient building or temple in the village it should be retained and preserved. In addition to what was said before, it may be noted that the temple for a deity may be built in addition to the quarters mentioned before. It can be at the head, foot, or middle of a street or in the interspace of two streets. Residential quarters can be grouped around the same. All the streets including the side once should confirm to the size and shape of the quarters they pass through. The entrance door of the houses in a village should generally be constructed on the south side. However the door in a house should follow the special rule. The length of the house on the side of a street being divided into nine parts, there should be left, both in the exterior and interior, five parts on the right side and out of the remaining four parts, three should be left on the left side. In the remaining one part the entrance door should be made. Otherwise the entrance door may be on the left side of the middle line of the house.

Re-planning a Village

In the case of replanning a village, the architect or town planner should follow the order laid down for all villages. If the expansion of a village take place towards the east and south direction it is good. It is less, if it happens to south and west. However expansion can be affected in all directions provided if the original land area is intact and customs of the time and place is still being followed.

The region by the two sides of a street should be furnished with stalls. The houses in the street can range from one storey to twelve storeys. Whether high or low there must be uniformity in the height of the houses. All the big houses may have many storeys. The homes of inferior castes should have one storey only.

CHAPTER 3

IDEAL TOWN AND CAPITAL PLANNING

The planning of towns, cities, forts, and capitals in their layout plans is an extension of design of villages. As described in Sthāpatya Veda, towns, cities, forts, and capitals though they do not differ much in their basic set-up each do have some variation depending upon the location, population, and the royal residence etc. Besides it depends upon the status or type of rulers who stay there.

Cities with the Residences of Rulers

There are nine categories of such cities. They have number of sub-divisions. Their minimum dimension in width, starts with 400 rods and ends in 1000 rods. Again each of these has three sub-sections such as small, middle, and large. The nomenclature of each type of city are on the basis of ruler who resides in. The nine types of rulers are–Aṣṭragrahiṇ, Praharārka, Paṭṭābhaj, Maṇḍalesa, Paṭṭādhara, Parshnika, Narendra, Mahārājā, and Chakravartin. All names of cities are according to the status of the ruler who reside there.

Aṣṭragrahin

There are seven varieties in this type of city. Each has three variations as said before. They are as follows:

	Rods	*No.*
Ist	100-100-200	3
IInd	200-100-300	3
IIIrd	300-100-500	3
IVth	400-100-600	3
Vth	500-100-700	3

VIth	600-100-800	3
VIIth	700-100-900	3
VIIIth	800-100-1000	3
IXth	900-100-1100	3
Xth	1000-100-1200	3

Similarly each type of capital cities have difference in their total numbers. They are as under as per the Ruler as named below:

Aṣṭragrahin	=	30
Praharārka	=	21
Paṭṭābhaj	=	63
Maṇdalesa	=	63
Paṭṭādhara	=	63
Parshnika	=	63
Narendra	=	63
Mahārājā	=	63
Chakravartin	=	63

Besides these cities with royal residences, there are another varieties of cities. They are known as Nagar, Kevala (these two are cities without royal residences), Nagara, Pura, Nagarī, Kheṭa, Kharvaṭa, Kubjaka, and Pattana. All with name Nagara can also come under forts. Which is described following the above cities, are as follows–Sivirta or Vahinimukha, Sthaniya, Dronaka, Samviddha, Kolaka, Nigama and Skandhavara.

Site for a City with Royal Palace

It is preferable to plan a city of this type on the bank of a river. It should have the royal palace and Viṣṇu temple at the centre.

Kevala

This city should have four gates at the four cardinal points provided with a gopuras. There must be quarters for guards adjacent to the gates. There must be well equipped army barracks too, near the gates. The city should have large number of wealthy merchants residing in it. It should have number of markets inside it. All round there should be numerous temples with crowds of people of every sort.

Pura

A city without royal palace. It should have lot of gardens and orchards, possess dwellings of various castes and people. It must be a centre of trade and commerce and should have number of temples for worship.

Nagarī

A city situated near a river or a mountain. Inhabited by Śūdras. It should have a fencing wall for protection.

Kharvaṭa

This type of city is to be set up on the uplands, having lot of pasture lands around. Its population is a mixed one.

Kubjaka

It is a type of city in between Kheṭa and Kharvaṭa. All types of people reside in it. It does not have any protecting wall around it.

Pattana (Citadel)

A city located near a river. A centre of commerce having export and import trade. It has a mixed population. A city where trade in jewellry, silk, cloth, camphor etc., abound.

Sivira (Camp)

An outpost centre with lot of army establishments.

Senā or Mukhya Vahini

A city having various defence establishments. It has a royal palace within it. Have diverse population.

Sthaniya (Strategical city)

A city situated on a mountain with many types of defence establishments. Having a king's residence.

Droṇa (Straw)

A city built on the banks of a river very near to the sea. It has mixed population, a place of commerce.

Saṁviddhā

A city resided by Brahmins. Situated very near to a village. Having a small village within it.

Kolaka

If a Saṁviddhā type of city has a royal palace too it is known as Kolaka.

Skandhāvara

It is situated near a river and its inhabitants are mostly Kṣhatriyas. It has terraced garden and houses near the river.

Chārī

Same like that of Skandhāvara except that its residents are Brahmins and Vaiśyas. It has a royal palace.

Forts

There are seven types of forts. They are: Mountain fort, Forest fort, Water fort, Clay fort, Chariot fort, Divine fort, and Misra fort.

Mountain Fort

These are of three types. One built on a mountain other near a mountain and another surrounded by mountains and valleys.

Forest Fort

It is to be situated connected to a river. But it should have its entrance on the top.

Water Fort

A fort situated in an island either in a river or sea.

Clay Fort

A fort having mountain caves for the safety of the ruler to be secured from enemies. A king is expected to stay in such a fort.

Chariot Fort

It is a jail to imprison thieve. It is situated away from a village on plain open land, devoid of trees and water.

Divine Fort

It is a fort which can be defended effectively from enemies by an efficient defensive system at the entrance and exit areas.

Misra Fort

A fort situated in a place having mountains and forests.

All forts should have surrounding walls, and ditches should have strong gates at both the entrance and exit areas. Forts should built with bricks or stones. It should have walls 12 cubic foot high (18 feet) with gang ways half way from the bottom of the wall.

CHAPTER 4

VṚKṢHA ĀYURVEDA (Trees, Shrubs and Herbs Prescribed in Sthāpatya Ved)

According to Sthāpatya Ved it is imperative to know about other various valuable effects to the environment given out by various types of trees, plants, shrubs and herbs etc. This has been studied methodically and their effects to human physiology have been stated. This is effectively used in planning a garden around a home, planting trees around a village, public gardens and tree in the cities. The trees and plants have been classified according to the location of their use.

Gardens in a home should be on the left side or inside. The plants useful for indoor and outdoor (garden) are discussed here.

Indoor Plants

Champā, kund, chamelī, belā, nirwalika (narmudi), jāti, ketkī (yellow flower), white rose, karni, vasaul latā, jambir, badri, pooj, madhup, and jambu.

Outdoor Plants

(Gardens)—Champak, aśoka, punnāg, mango, tilak, shatpatika, bakul, dhattur, kamdal, shala, tal, taval, mamvas (agar), mandar (madar), pandrum (panja), mahuā, kadalī, chandan (sandal wood), vāt, ashwath, pathya, śiva (sāmī), imilī (tamarind), aloka, kadaṃb, nimb, padim, karpur, aguru, kumshuk, hayasipu (vanell), nāgalatā (nagnal), beejnimrat (bijoor), tintuki (ebony), and langli (jal pīpal).

TREES AND PLANTS THAT ARE GOOD OR BAD TO BE NEAR A HOME

Name of trees/Plants	*Good*	*Bad*	*Effect/Location*
Thorny trees		Bad	
Champā, rose, plantain, Chamelī and Ketaki	Good		
Milky trees, Baniyan, and pīpal. Trees with red flowers, trees with thorns, semer, pakkad, and gullar		Bad	Southeast that bring death
Punnāg, phalini, nīm, dhadim, aśoka, mālatī, nagakesar, javakusum, kesar, jayantī, chandan, bacha, aparijitha, madhuka, bel, mango, dālchīnī, nagar and coconut	Good		Any where any corner
Pīpal, kadaṃb, plantain, citrus			Where they exist those houses do not prosper
Kaṭhal (jack fruit tree)	Good		Any where
All trees			South
Thorny trees			Creates enemys
Milky trees			Destroy wealth
Flowering trees			Affects progeny
Plants with yellow flowers			Not good near homes
Pakkad			North South
Baniyan			East West
Gullar			South North
Pīpal			West East

However if these trees are combined with trees like, punnāg, aśoka, arist, baniyan, jack tree, sāmī, or sāl and is at the centre of these it is not bad.

Fertilizers

The method of fertilizing and watering plants and trees for better yield are as below.

Kelthi, urad, moong or jau, any one of these pulses or grain should be boiled in water. This water when cool is to be applied at the root of the plants/trees to help them to bear abundant flowers and fruits.

Trees (to be planted around a village)

Guller, pīpal tree, bas, imilī (tamarind), chandan, jambuphal (jāmun), kadaṃb, aśoka, bakul, bilv (aegle marmalos), awala, kaith, rajadan, ām (mango), punnāg, toodkashtha, anār (pomogranate), akhroṭ (walnut), bhissat, sheesham, khirnee, khajūr, devakran, phalgu (aṅjīr), tapicha (tamal), simbal, kuddāl, louvely (hafare vadi), dhatri, kārmuk (betal nut), matulung (bisoora nīṁbū), lakuch (badhal), nārial (coconut), kelā, etc.

TWIGS FROM PLANTS/TREES GOOD FOR CLEANING OF TEETH

Name in Hindi	*Botanical Name*	*Benefit*
Vikankata	Gymrasporia spinosa	Spiritual splendor
Bilva	Aegal marmalos	Spiritual splendor
Kashmari	Gmelina arborea	Spiritual splendor
Ksema		Good wife
Arka	Calotropis gigntea	Great brilliance/ power
Madhuk	Gynometra ramiflora	Virtuous sons and prosperity
Sirish	Albizzia lebbeck	Fortune
Karanj	Pongamia pinnata	Fortune
Plaksa	Ficus arnottiana	Abundant wealth
Jātī	Jasminum officinale	Honour and respect
Asvattha	Ficus religious	Prominence
Badari	Lizyphus jujuba	Good health and long life
Bṛhatī	Solanum xanthocaspum	Good health and long life
Khadira	Acacia catechu	Wealth and power
Ati Muktaka	Ovgeinia dalbergioides	Desired objects

Name in Hindi	*Botanical Name*	*Benefit*
Nipa	Anthocephalus indicum	Wealth
Karavira	Nerium indicus	Plenty of good
Sāmī	Prospis spicigara	Plenty of good
Arjuna	Terminalia arjuna	Food, help to destroy enemy
Syama	Echinochloa frumentacea	Food, help to destroy enemy
Sāla	Shora robusta	Respectability
Asvakarna	Vatica robusta	Respectability
Devadaru	Cedrus devadaru	Respectability
Atarvsaka	Adhatoda vasica	Respectability
Priyangu	Aglaia Rox burghiana	Becomes Favourite of all
Apamarga	Achyranthes aspera	Becomes Favourite of all
Jambu	Syzygium jambos	Becomes favourite of all

Tooth Stick

One should use a good tooth stick after good desire for well being in the coming year. Sitting at ease, facing north or east with a calm mind. After the tooth cleaning is over, wash the stick well and keep it in a clean place.

TIMBER OF TREES SUITED FOR PILLARS, BEAMS, COUCHES, BEDSTEAD, CARS, CHARIOTS, TOOTH PICK

Name in Hindi	*Botanical Name*	*Purpose of use*
Khadira	Acacia catechu	Pillar
Puti padapa (Pine tree)		Pillar
Hema padapa (Pine tree)		Pillar
Kshirni (Milk tree)		Pillar

Name in Hindi	*Botanical Name*	*Purpose of use*
Karmuka (Betal nut tree)		Upper beam
Venu reed		Reed mixed with bamboo cane. Bamboo cane should be long and straight.
Bakula		Suited for frames and bedsteads for the frames etc., of couches as well as for their boards.
Asvini pentra		Suited for frames and bedsteads for the frames etc., of couches as well as for their boards.
Drakhsa		Suited for frames and bedsteads for the frames etc., of couches as well as for their boards.
Red sandal		Suited for frames and bedsteads for the frames etc., of couches as well as for their boards.
Nimba		Suited for frames and bedsteads for the frames etc., of couches as well as for their boards.
Chandana	Santalum album	Suited for frames and bedsteads for the frames etc., of couches as well as for their boards.

Name in Hindi	*Botanical Name*	*Purpose of use*
Chapa		Suited for frames and bedsteads for the frames etc., of couches as well as for their boards.
Saku		Suited for frames and bedsteads for the frames etc., of couches as well as for their boards.
Sāmī		Suited for frames and bedsteads for the frames etc., of couches as well as for their boards.
Daṇḍa		Suited timber for the legs of all couches.
Kshirini (Milk tree)		Suited timber for the legs of all couches.
Tinduka		Suited timber for the legs of all couches.
Virala		Suited timber for the legs of all couches.
Saka		Suited timber for the legs of all couches.
Chandana	Santalum album	Beds and couches.
Asana	Bridelia moutane	Beds and couches.
Spandana		Beds and couches.
Harida	Coscinium fennstratum	Beds and couches.
Deodaru	Pinus devadaru	Beds and couches.
Tinduki	Diospyros paniculata	Beds and couches.
Shala	Shora robusta	Beds and couches.
Kasmari	Gmelina arborea	Beds and couches.

Anjana	Moringa deifera	Beds and couches.
Padmaka	Prunus cerasoides	Beds and couches.
Shaka	Tectona grandis	Beds and couches.
Simsapa	Dalbergia sissoo	Beds and couches.
Sriparani	Gamalina arborea	Cot made woolly of this bestows wealth.
Asana	Terminalia tomentosa	Cot made woolly of this destroys diseases.
Pith of tintuka	Diospyros paniculala	Cot made woolly of this leads to wealth.
Chandana	Santalum album	Destroy enemies and bestows religious merit, fame and long life.
Padmaka	Prunus cerasoides	Long life prosperity.
Sāla	Shorea robusta	Happiness and prosperity.
Shaka	Tectona grandis	Happiness and prosperity.

A king reposing on a cot made of sandal wood and covered with gold and bedecked with wonderful gems will be honoured even by Gods. A cot made of tinduka or simsapa along with some other timber will not yield good result. So is one of deodar or asana along with sriparna. The sāla and saka as well as haridraka and kadaṃba are good whether used jointly or separately. A cot wholly made of spandana or amba tree (in Marathis Ambada) is not auspicious. Since it destroys life. One of Asana coupled with some other timber results in all kinds of troubles. It is beneficial to have legs made out of spandana tree. Cots and seats made of any fruit tree will have favourable effects.

Illustrations of Architectural Plans

Erection of Gnomons and Pegs
Site Plans
Village Plans
Towns & Forts Plans

Erection of Gnomons and Pegs

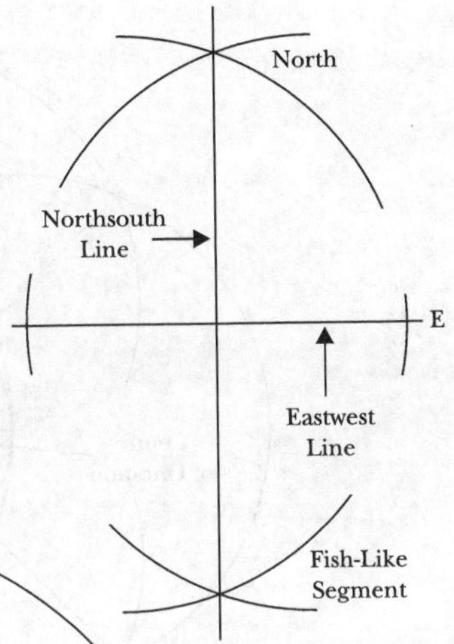

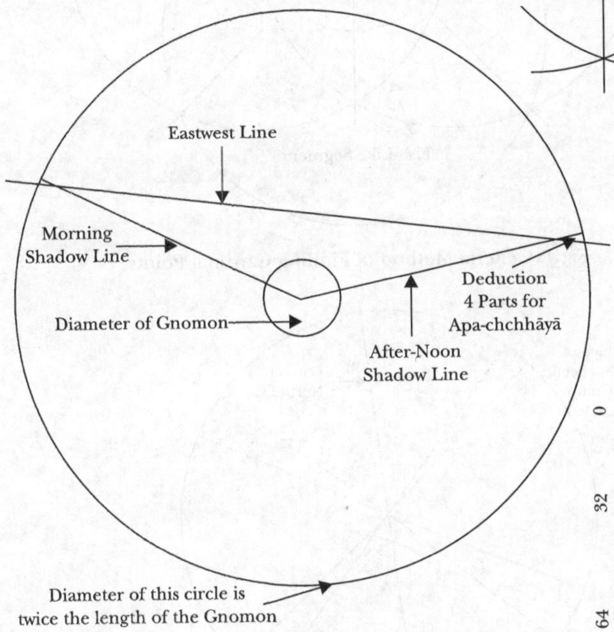

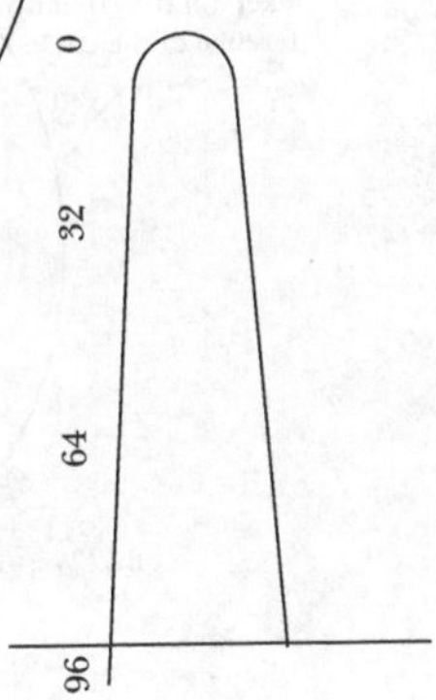

Shape of Gnomon

NOTE:
These figures are only applicable to the months of Vriśchika and Āshādha. The month of Mina having Apa-chchhāyā of 4 parts the shadow lines for morning etc., would decline towards the south.

Erection of Gnomons and Pegs

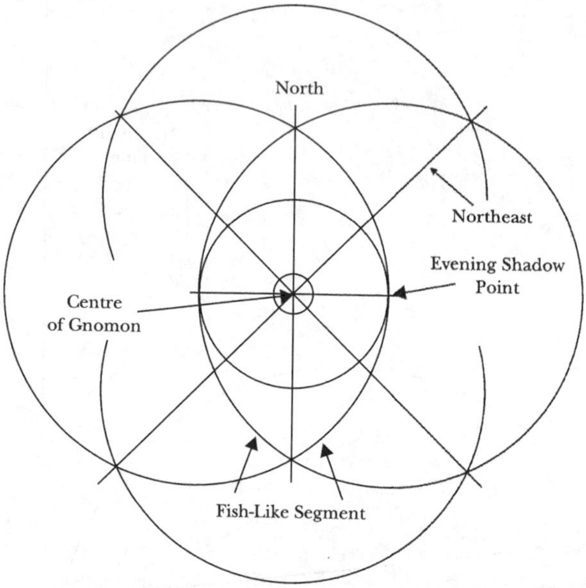

Fig.1: General Method of Finding Cardinal Points

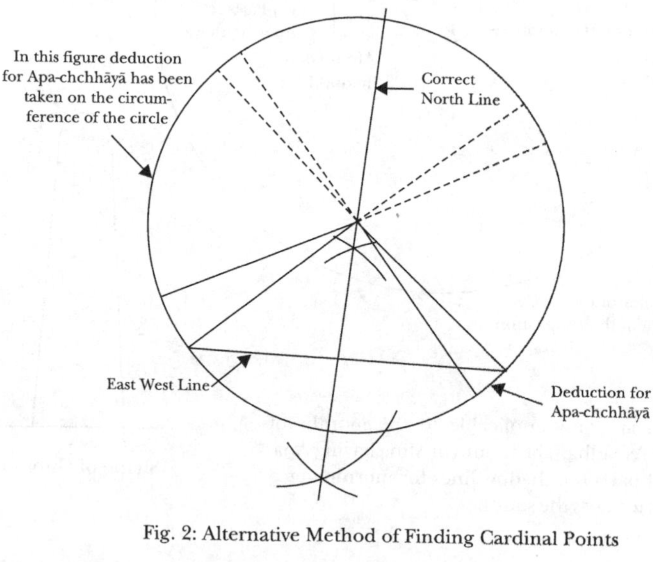

Fig. 2: Alternative Method of Finding Cardinal Points

Erection of Gnomons and Pegs

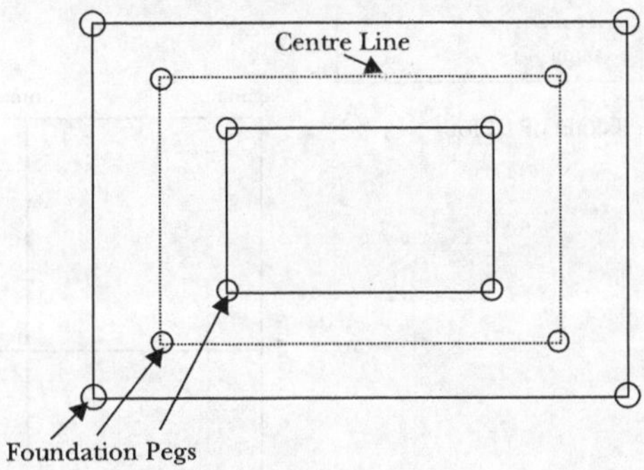

Fig. 3: Method of Fixing Foundation Pegs

Site Plans

(a) Sakala of 1 Plot, (b) Pechaka of 4 Plots,
(c) Pīṭha of 9 Plots

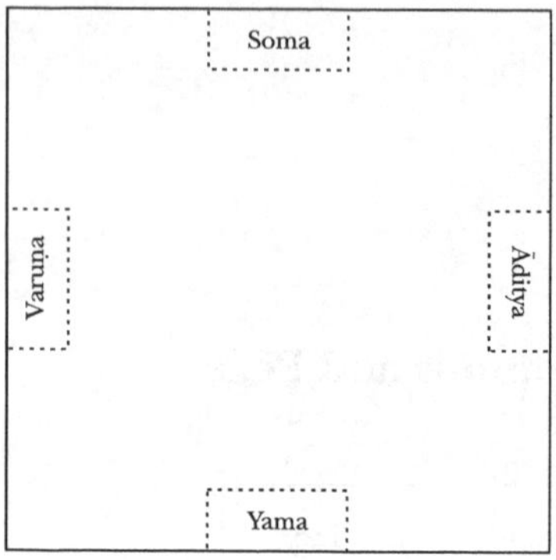

Fig. 1: Sakala of 1 Plot A

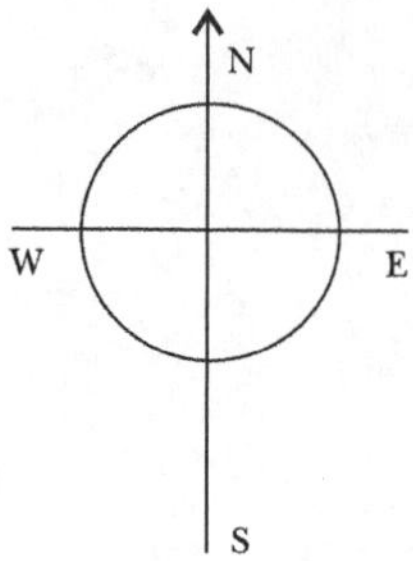

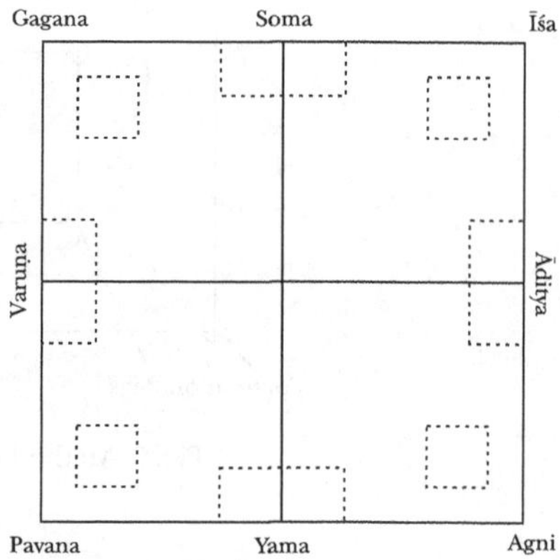

Fig. 2: Pechaka of 4 Plots B

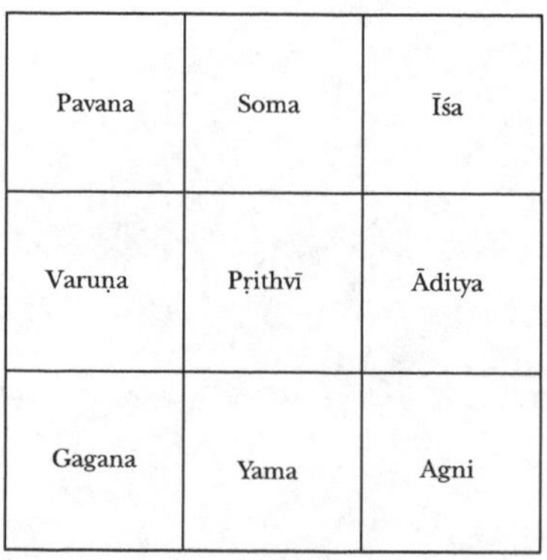

Fig. 3: Pīṭha of 9 Plots C

Site Plans

Mahāpiṭha of 16 Plots

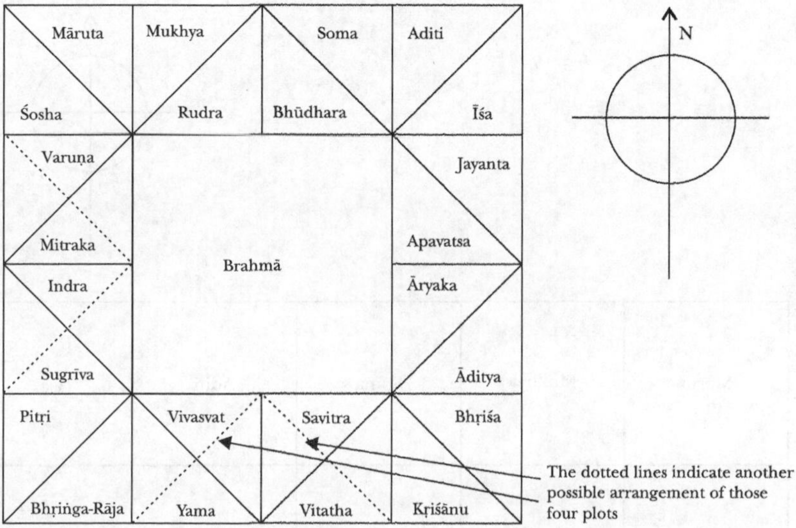

Fig. 1: Mahāpiṭha of 16 Plots

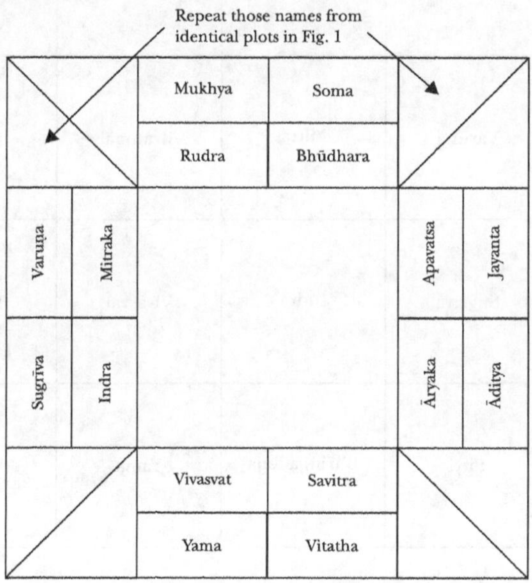

Fig. 1A: Mahāpiṭha of 16 Plots Arranged Differently

Site Plans

UPA-Pīṭha Plan of 25 Plots

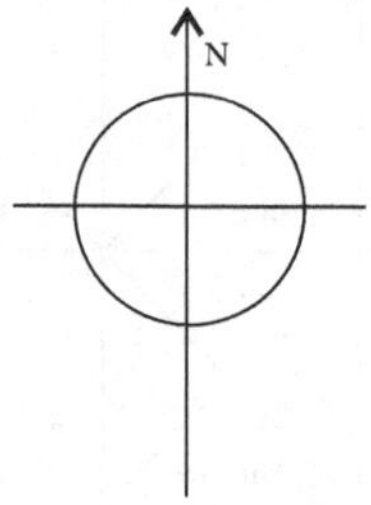

Marut	Mukhya	Soma	Aditi	Īśa
Śosha	Rudra	Bhūdhara	Apavatsa	Jayanta
Varuṇa	Mitra	Brahmā	Āryaka	Āditya
Sugrīva	Indra	Vivasvat	Savitra	Bhṛiśa
Pitṛi	Bhṛiṅga-Rāja	Yama	Vitatha	Agni

NOTE:
Detail allotments for this type have been obtained from "*Architecture of Manasara*", p. 37, footnote.

Site Plans

Ugra-Pīṭha Plan of 36 Plots

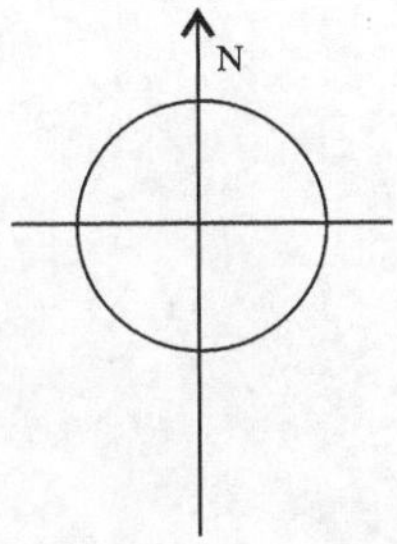

Vāyu	Mukhya	Soma	Aditi	Īśa
Śosha	Rudra	Bhūdhara	Apavatsa	Jayanta
Varuṇa	Mitra	Brahmā	Āryaka	Āditya
Sugrīva	Indra	Vivasvat	Savitra	Bhṛiśa
Pitṛi	Bhṛiṅga-Rāja	Yama	Vitatha	Agni

NOTE:
This is an amplification of the Ugra-Pīṭha Type.

Site Plans

Sthaṇḍila Plan of 49 Plots

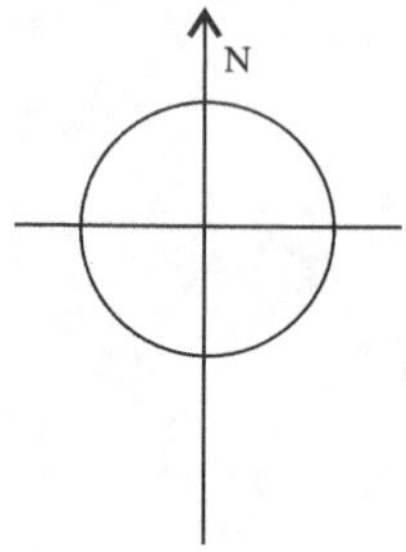

Vāyu	Mukhya	Soma	Aditi	Īśa
Śosha	Rudra	Bhūdhara	Apavatsa	Jayanta
Varuṇa	Mitra	Brahmā	Āryaka	Āditya
Sugrīva	Indra	Vivasvat	Savitra	Bhṛiśa
Pitṛi	Bhṛiṅga-Rāja	Yama	Vitatha	Agni

NOTE:
This is an amplification of the Ugra Pīṭha type.

Site Plans

Chaṇḍita Plan of 64 Plots

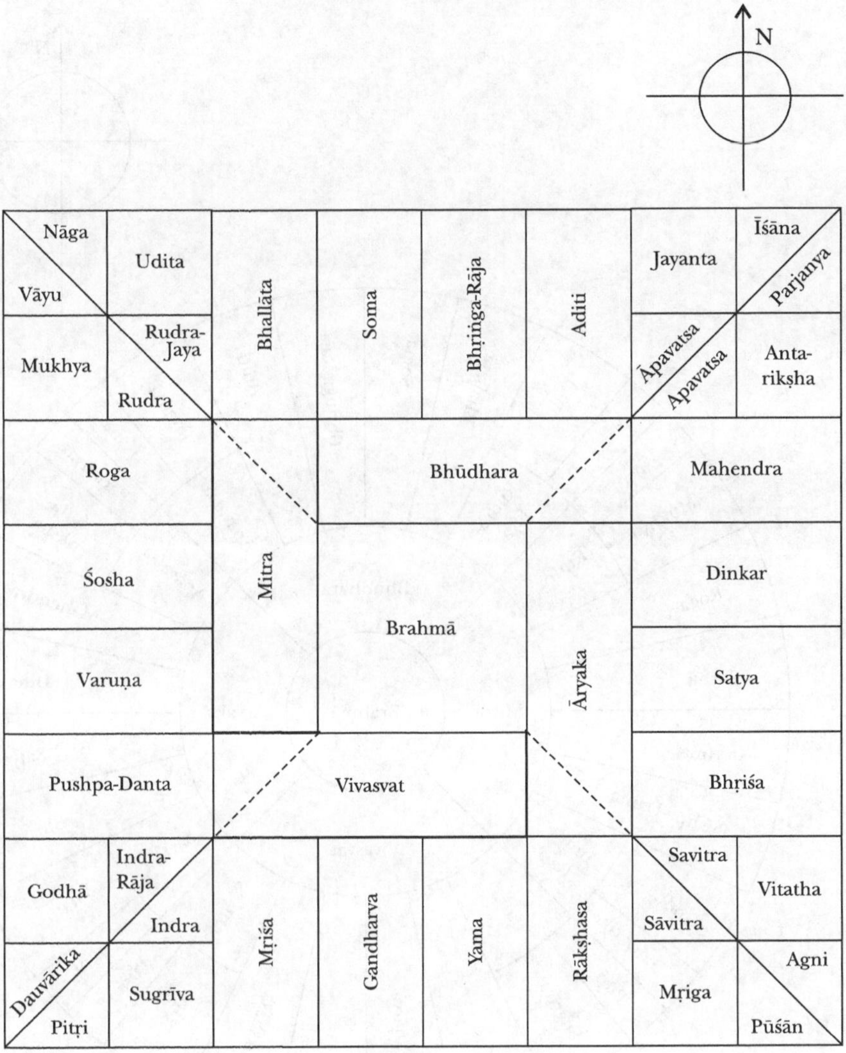

NOTE:

1. The dotted lines on the four corners of the Brahmā Plot indicate another arrangement of those four plots (Āryaka etc.).
2. Another alternative arrangement is possible by starting with Āryaka from the due northeastern plot of Brahmā.

Site Plans

Chaṇḍita Plan of 64 Plots

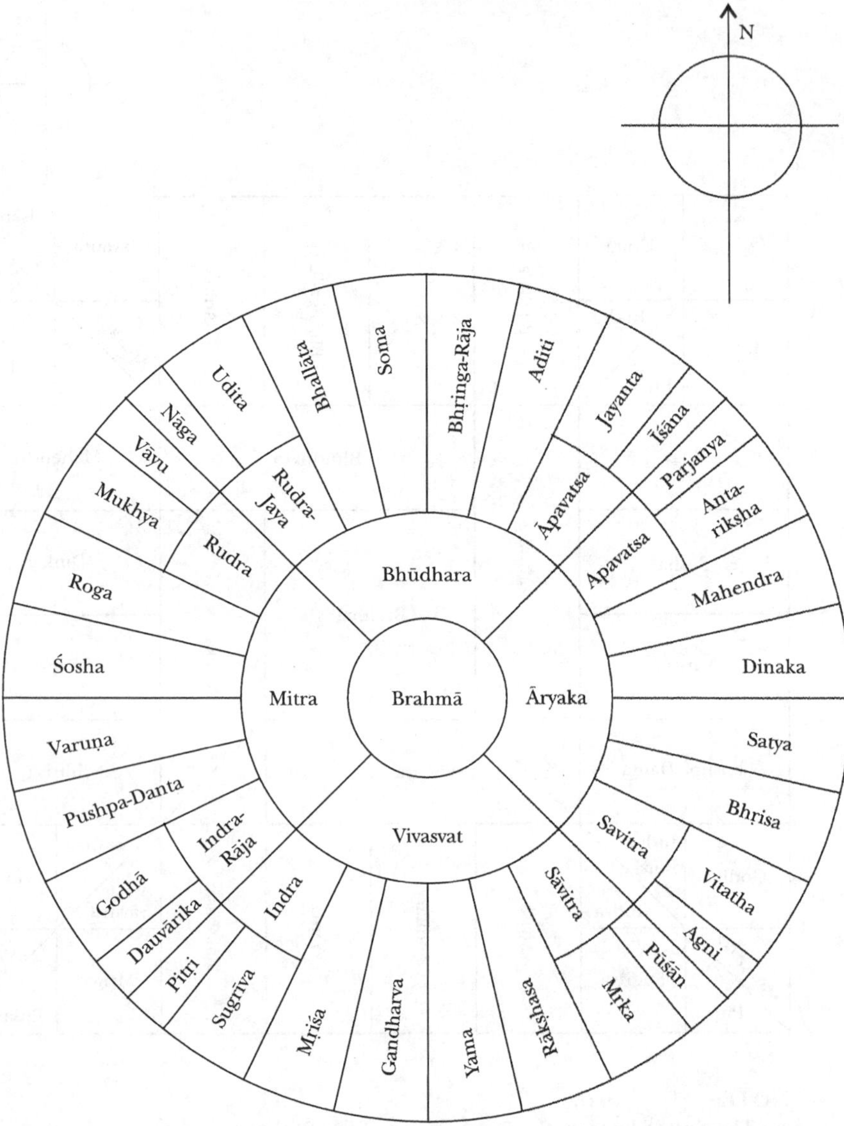

NOTE:
The idea of circular plans has been taken from "*Bṛihatsaṁhitā*", pp. 44-45, footnotes.

Site Plans

Paṛama-Śāyika Plan of 81 Plots

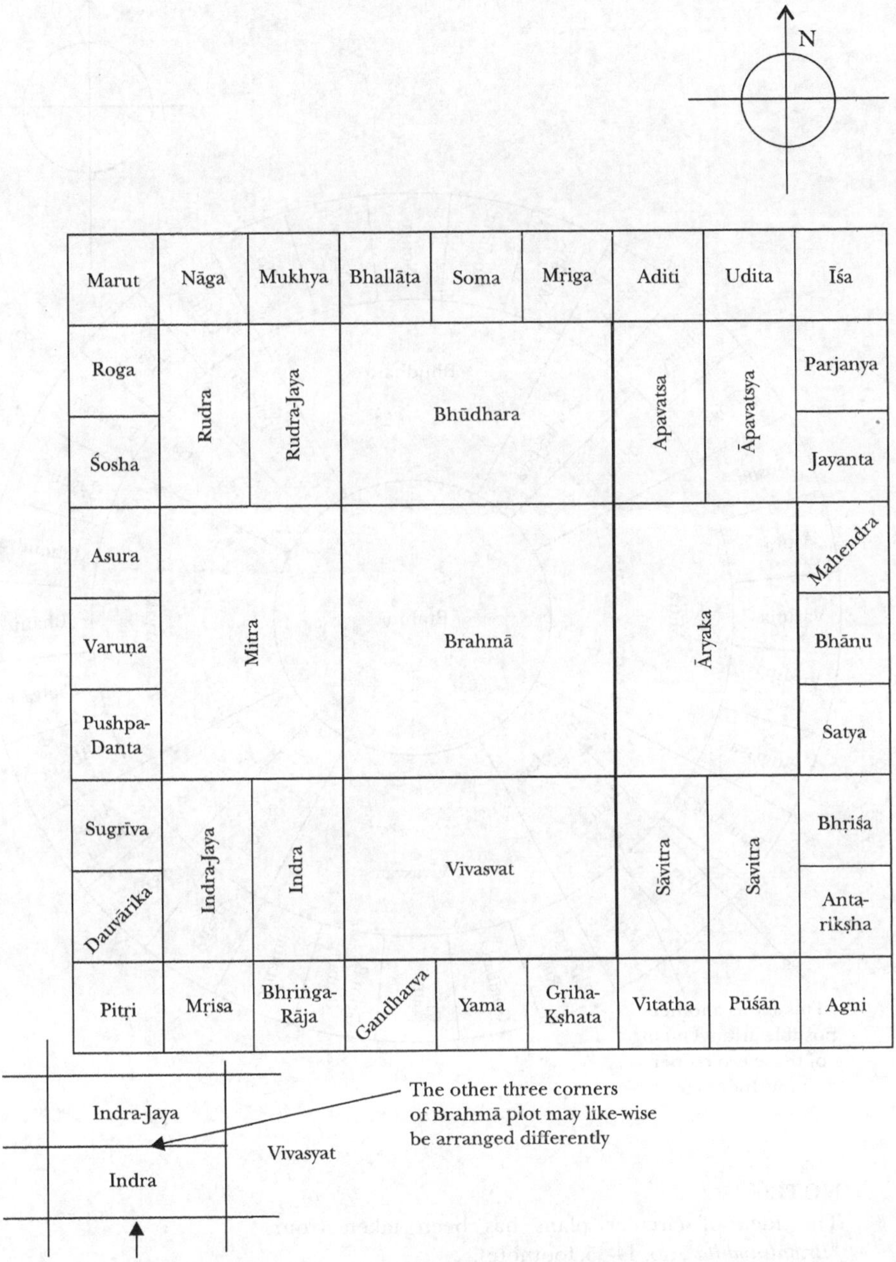

Alternative Arrangement

Site Plans

Paṛama-Śāyika Plan of 81 Plots

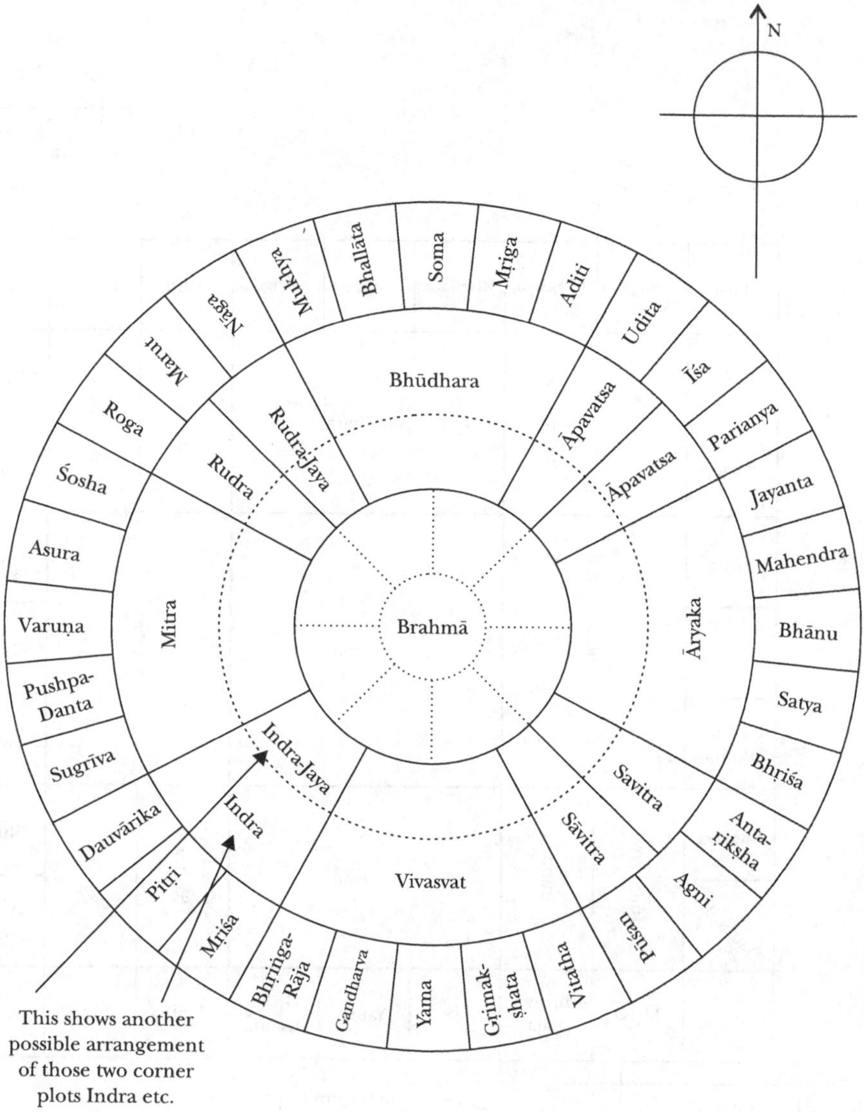

NOTE:

The idea of circular plans has been taken from "*Bṛihatsaṁhitā*", pp. 44-45, footnotes.

Site Plans

Parama-Śāyika Plan of 81 Plots

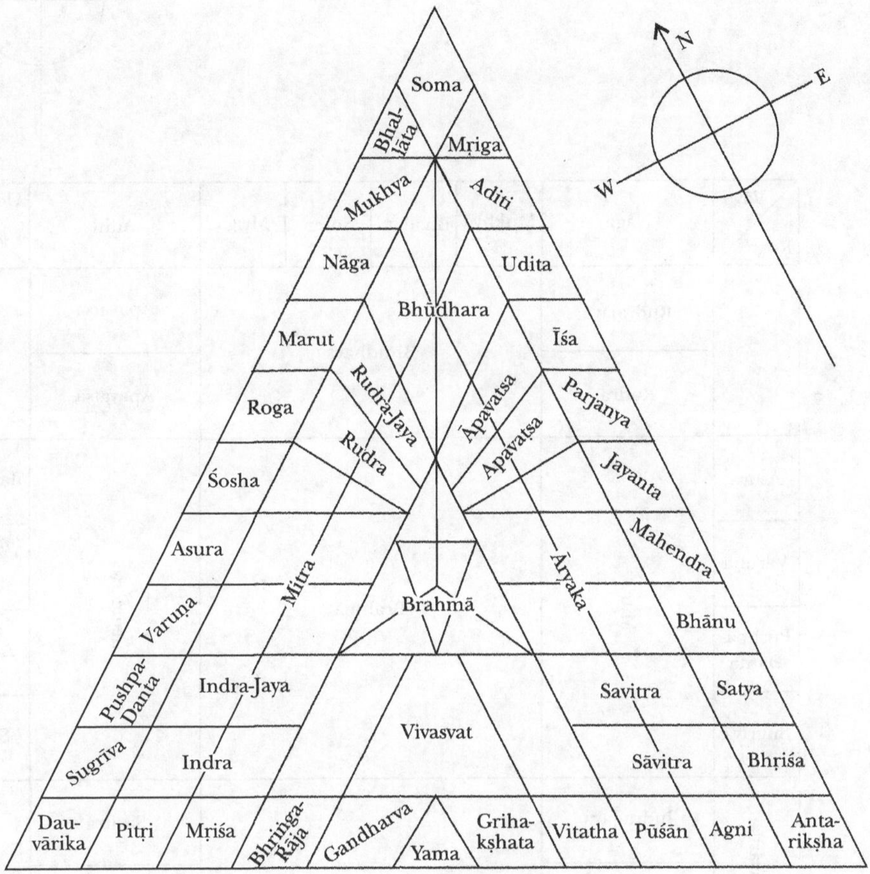

NOTE:
The idea of triangular plan has been obtained from Utpala.

Site Plans

Āsana Plan of 100 Plots

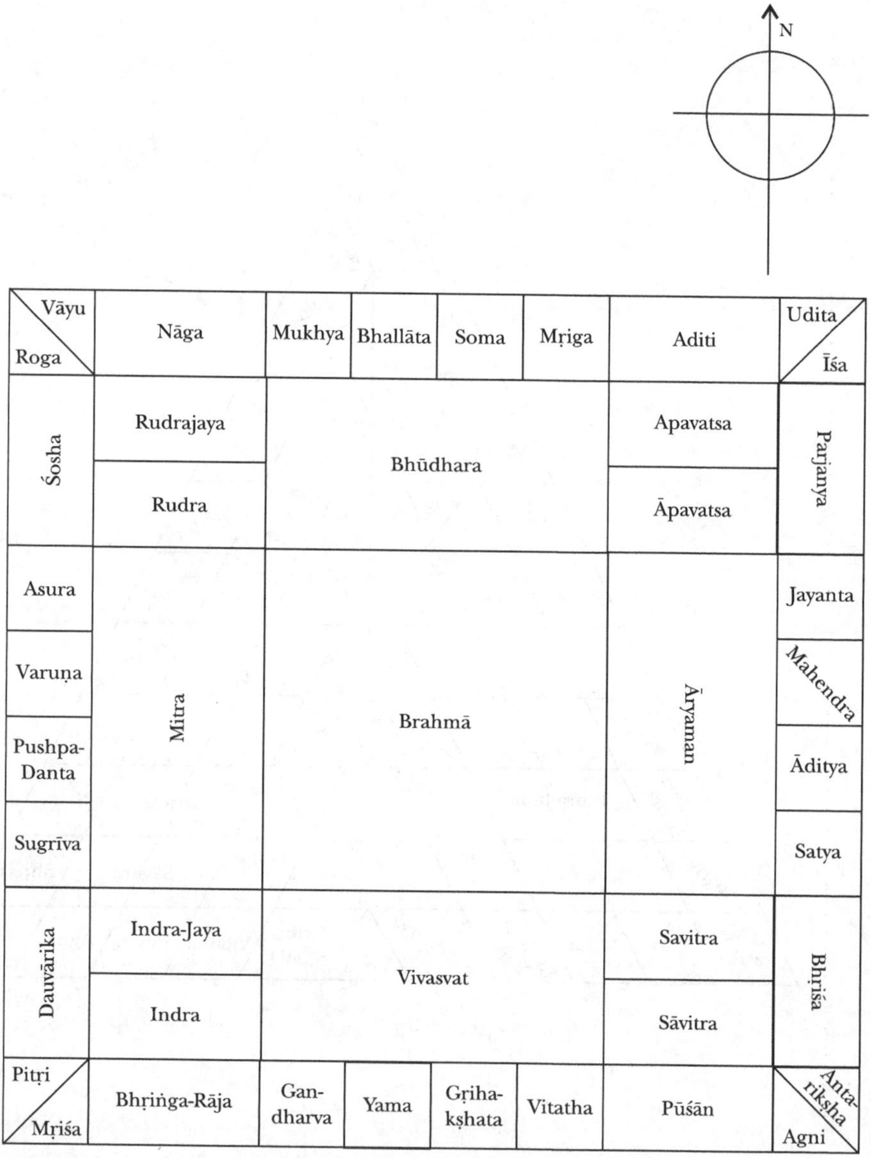

NOTE:

The details of this plan have been obtained from "*Silpa-Ratna*".

Site Plans

Āsana Plan of 100 Plots

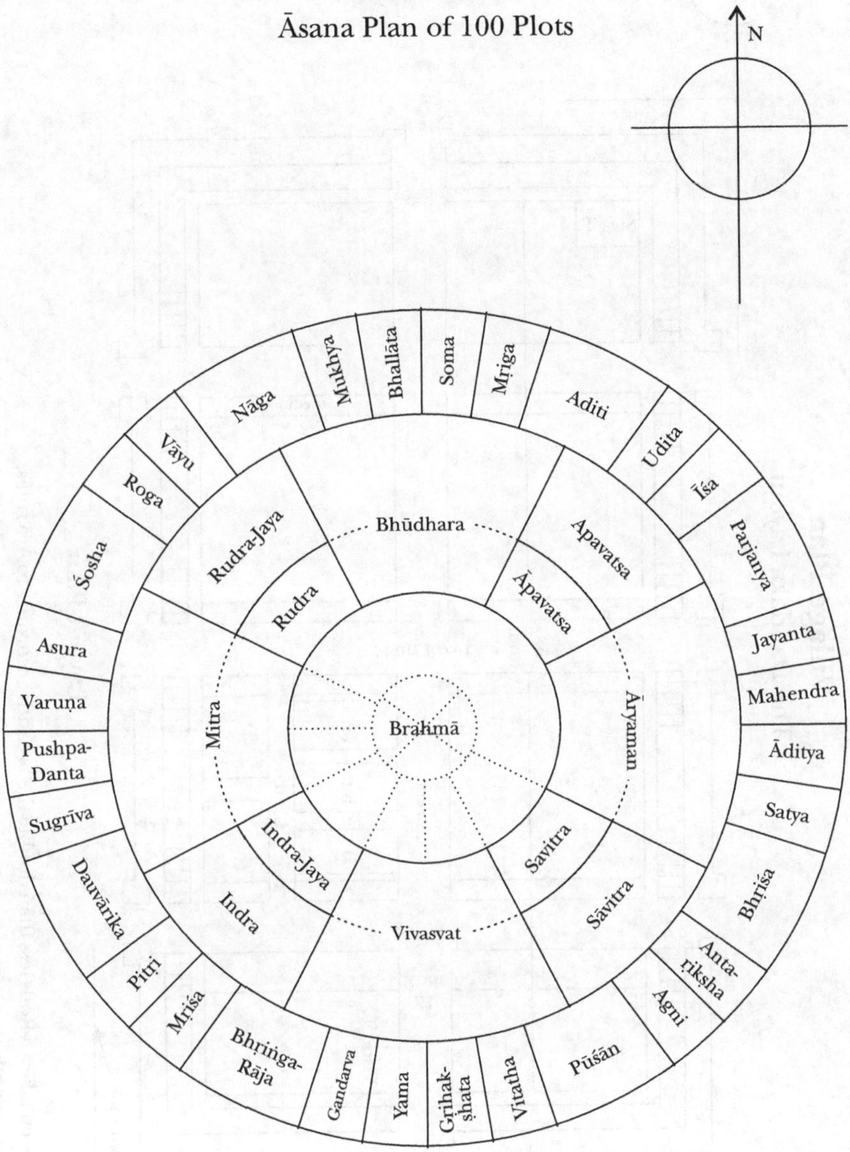

NOTE:
The idea of circular plans has been obtained from "*Bṛihatsahmitā*" and "*Śilpa-Ratna*".

Village Plan

The Dandaka Layout

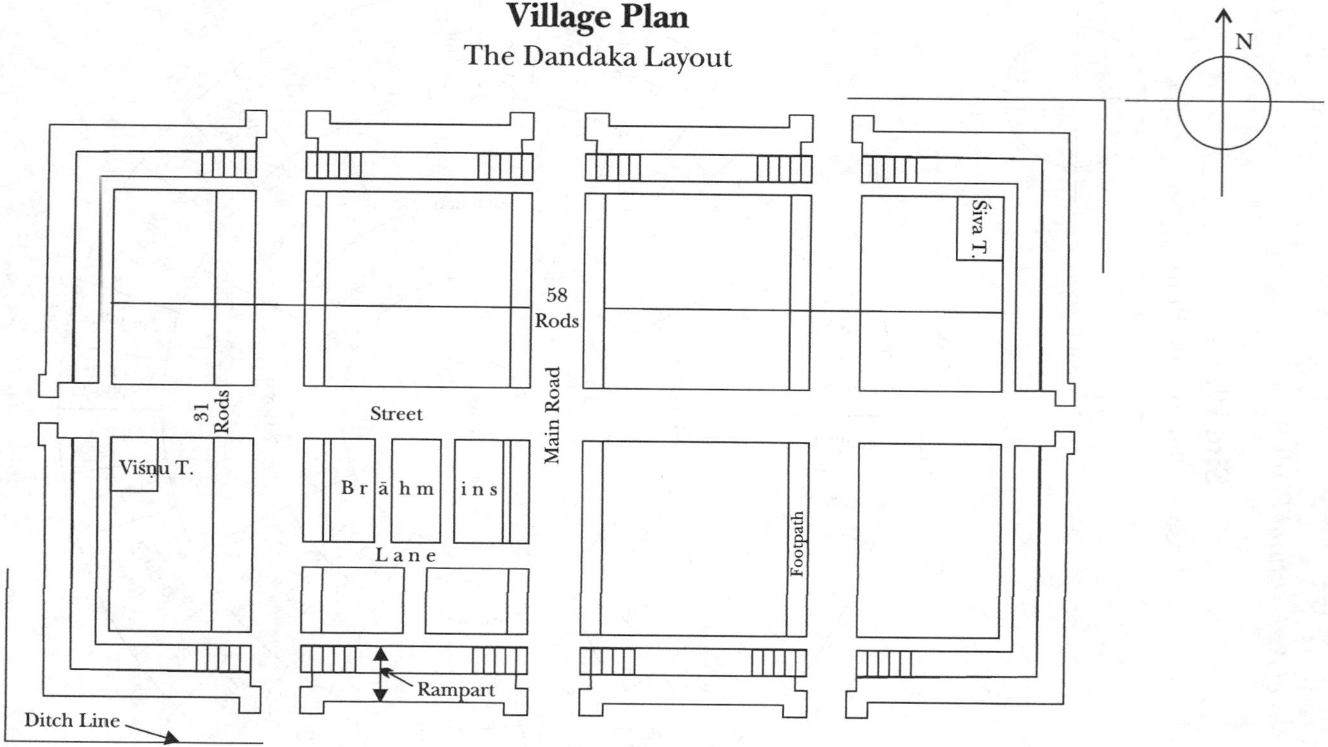

Layout Plan

NOTE:

The length has been taken 4 Rods less than double the breadth according to Āya rules.

'T' here stands for Temple.

Village Plan

The Sarvato-Bhadra Layout

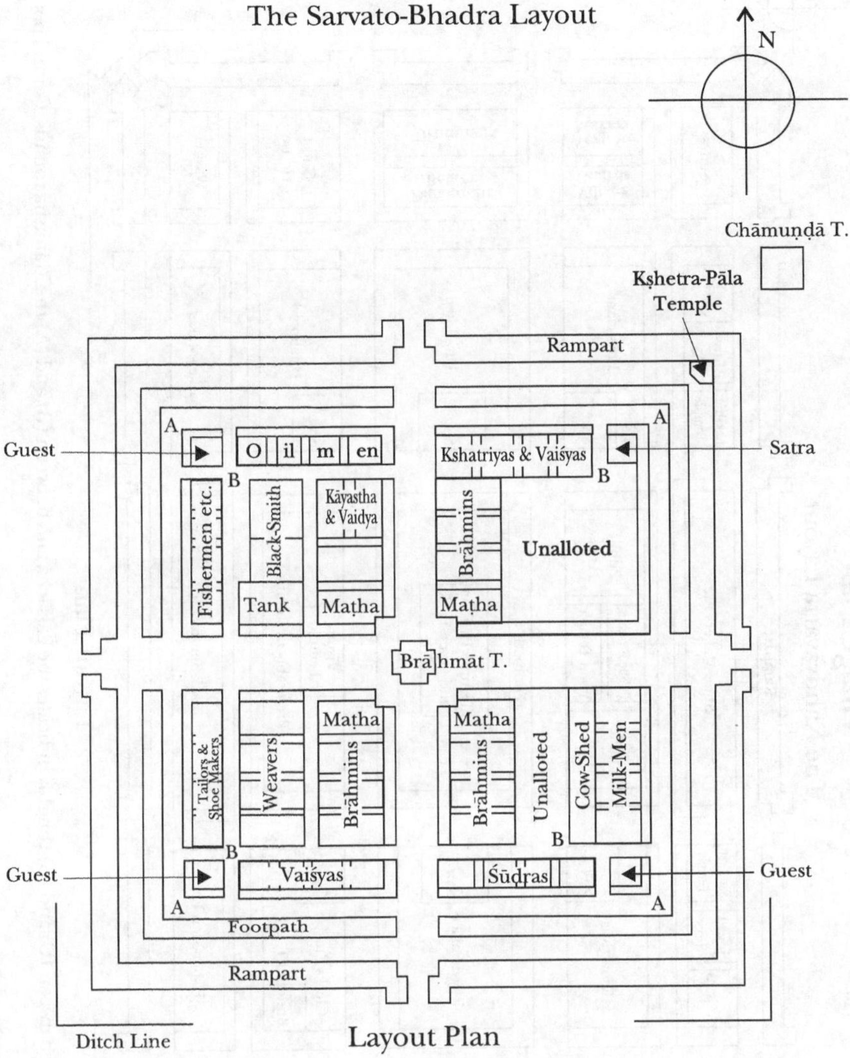

Layout Plan

NOTE:
The surrounding plot between (A) and (B) is the last or Paisachas round.
'T' stands for Temple.

Village Plan

The Nandyāvarta Layout

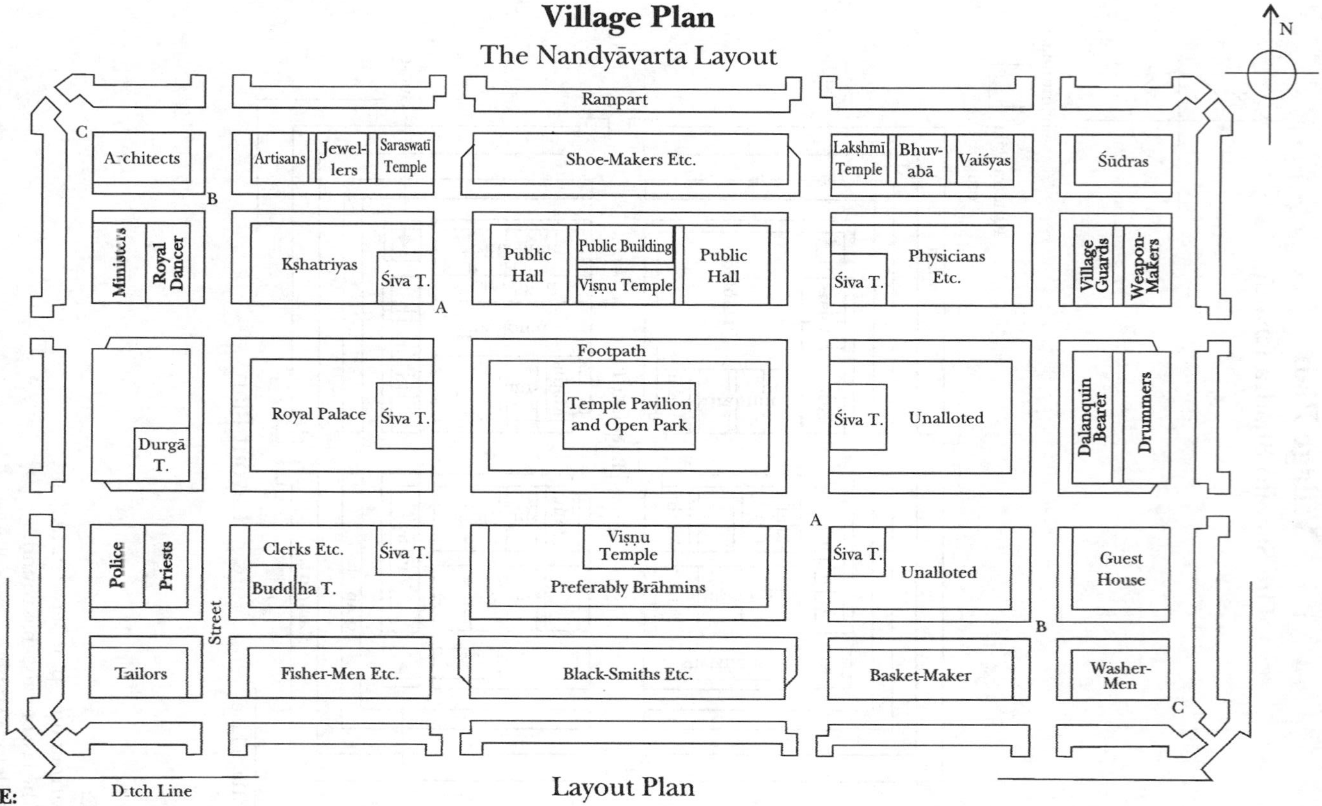

Layout Plan

NOTE:

The surrounding strip of plot between (C) and (B) roughly indicates the Paiśācha and between (B) and (A) the Mānusha rounds. Central portion is the Daiva Plot.

'T' stands for Temple.

Village Plan

The Padmaka Layout

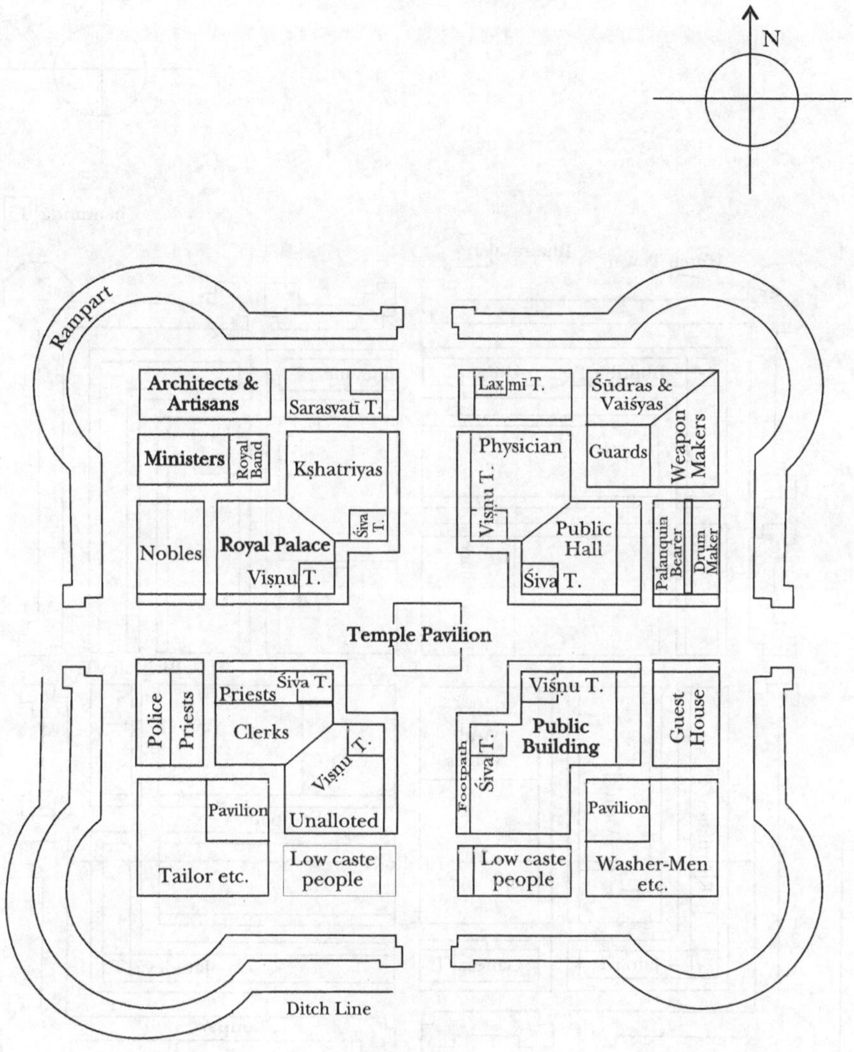

Layout Plan

NOTE:

The outer wall can be made circular hexagonal or octagonal.

'T' stands for Temple.

Village Plan

The Svastika Layout

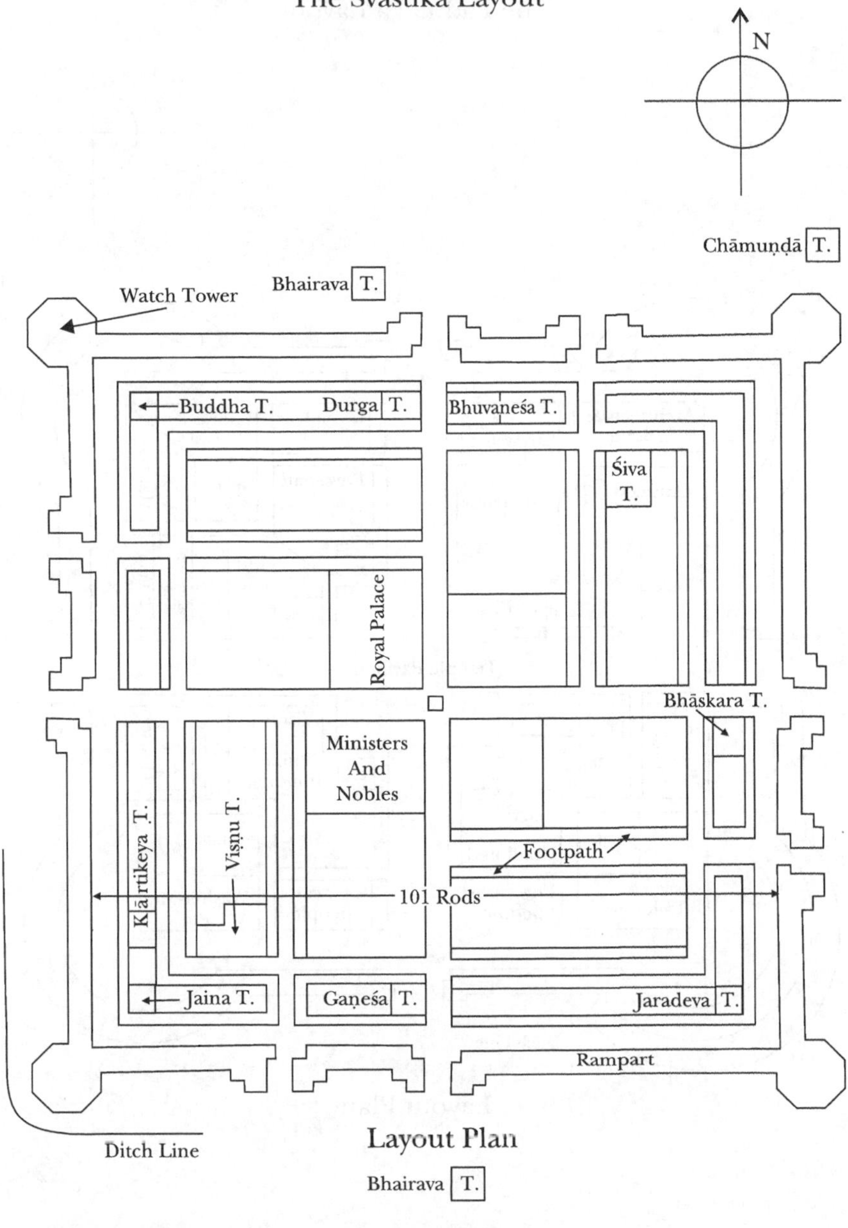

Layout Plan

NOTE:
Only the allotment of palaces for kings and nobles as well as of temples for gods has been given in the text. 'T' stands for Temple.

Village Plan

The Prastara Layout

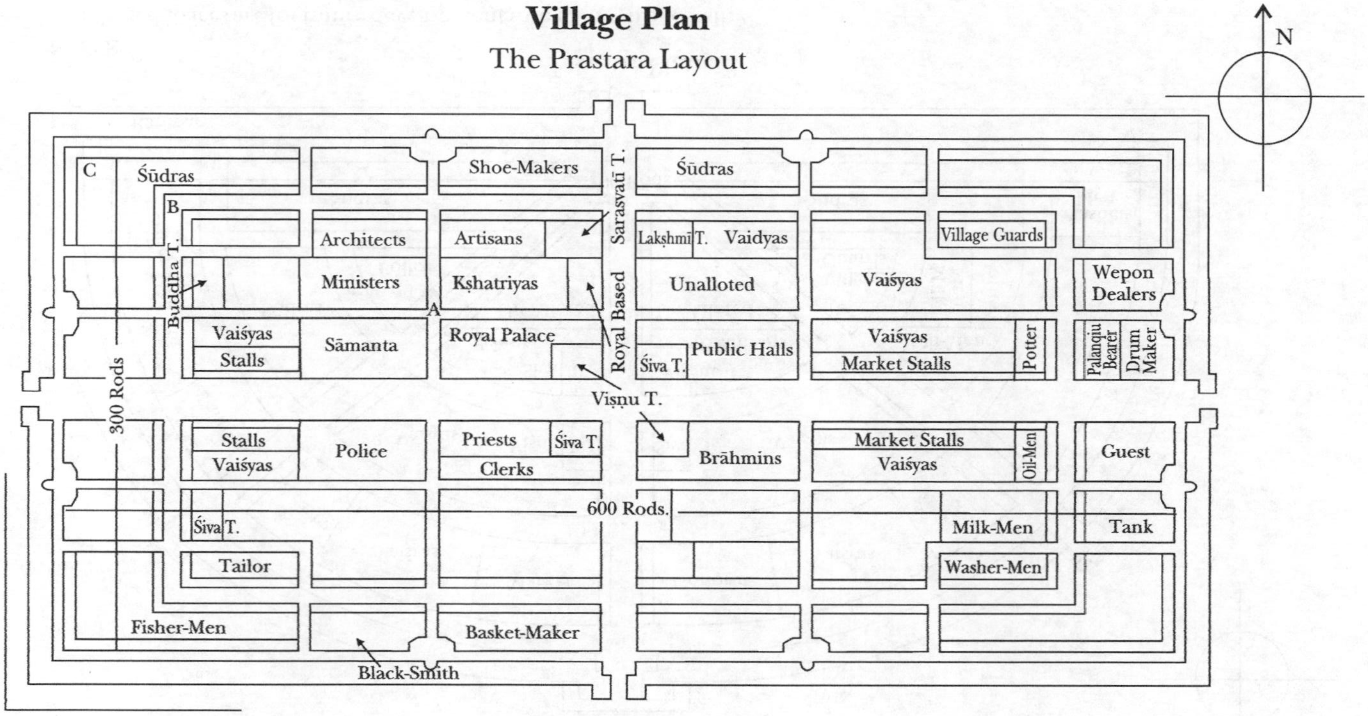

Layout Plan

NOTE:

The surrounding strip of plot between (C) and (B) roughly indicates the Paiśācha and between (B) and (A) the Mānusha rounds. Central portion is the Daiva Plot.

'T' stands for Temple.

Village Plan

The Kārmuka Layout

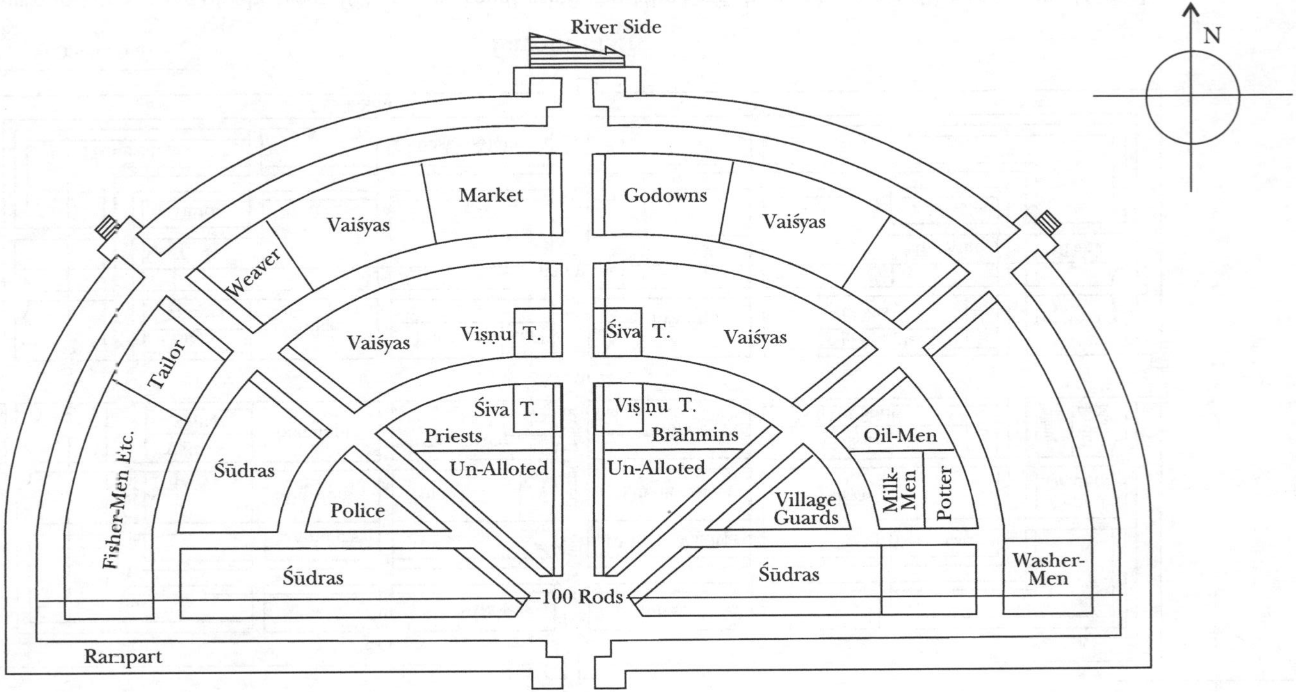

Layout Plan

NOTE:
Unallotted spaces are for future development with in the village wall.

Village Plan

The Chaturmukha Layout

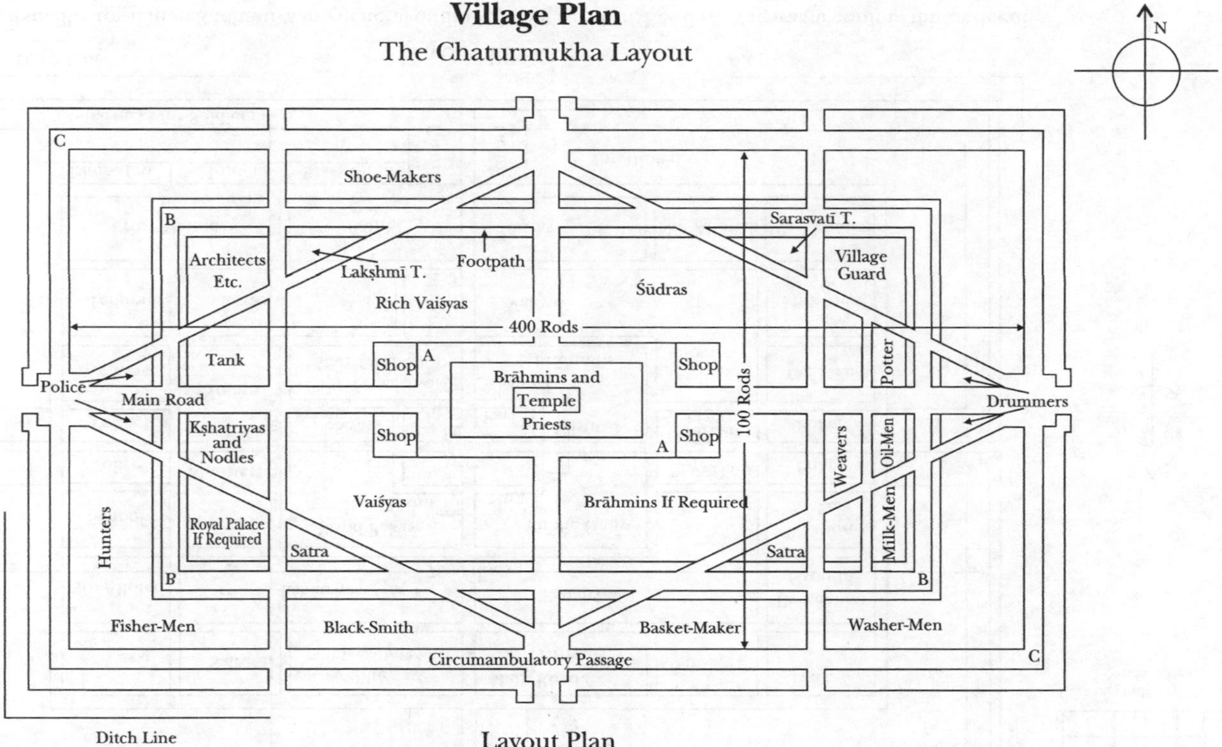

Layout Plan

NOTE:

The surrounding strip of plot between (C) and (B) roughly indicates the Paiśācha and between (B) and (A) the Mānusha rounds. Central portion is the Daiva Plot.

'T' stands for Temple.

This village is for the Vaisyas mainly.

Towns and Forts Plan

The Rājadhānīya Layout for Chakra-vartin Kings

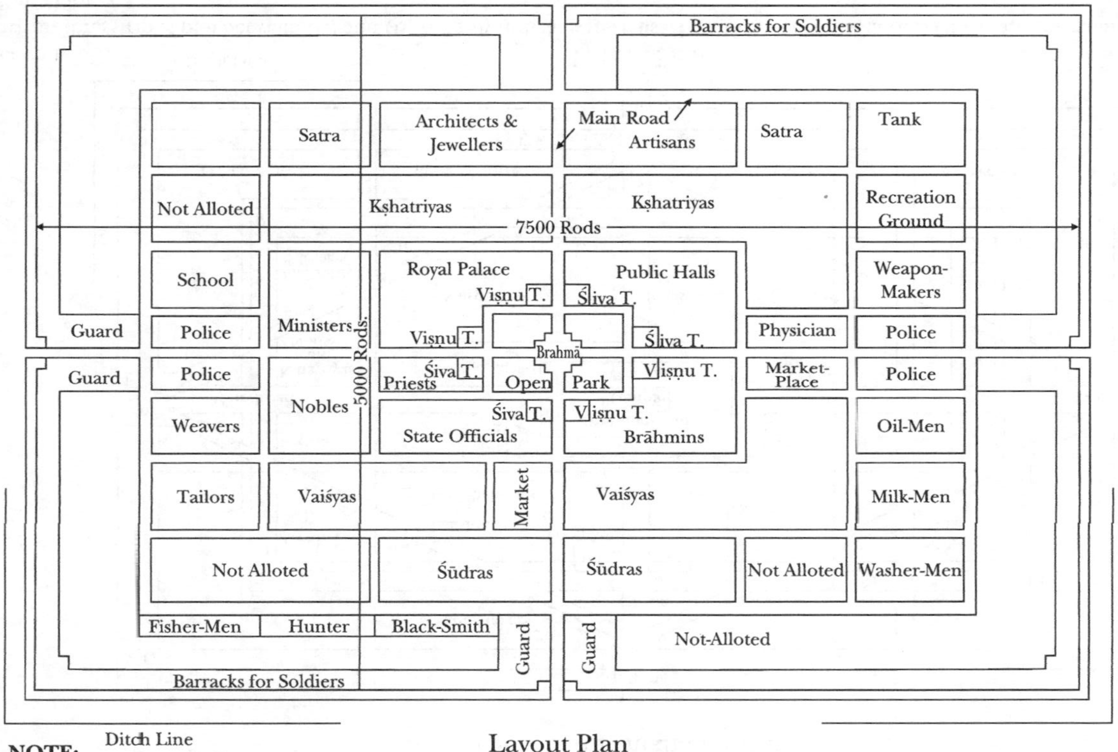

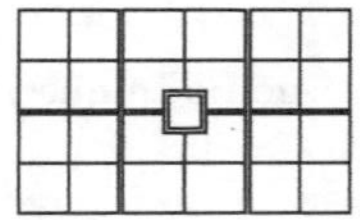

General Outline of Nagara
Not to Scale

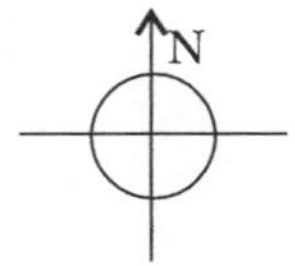

Layout Plan

NOTE:
Nagara is a smaller town than Rādhānīya so a general outline has been shown. Kevala & Nagara vary only in minor details.

Towns and Forts Plan

General Outline of Kharvaṭa Town

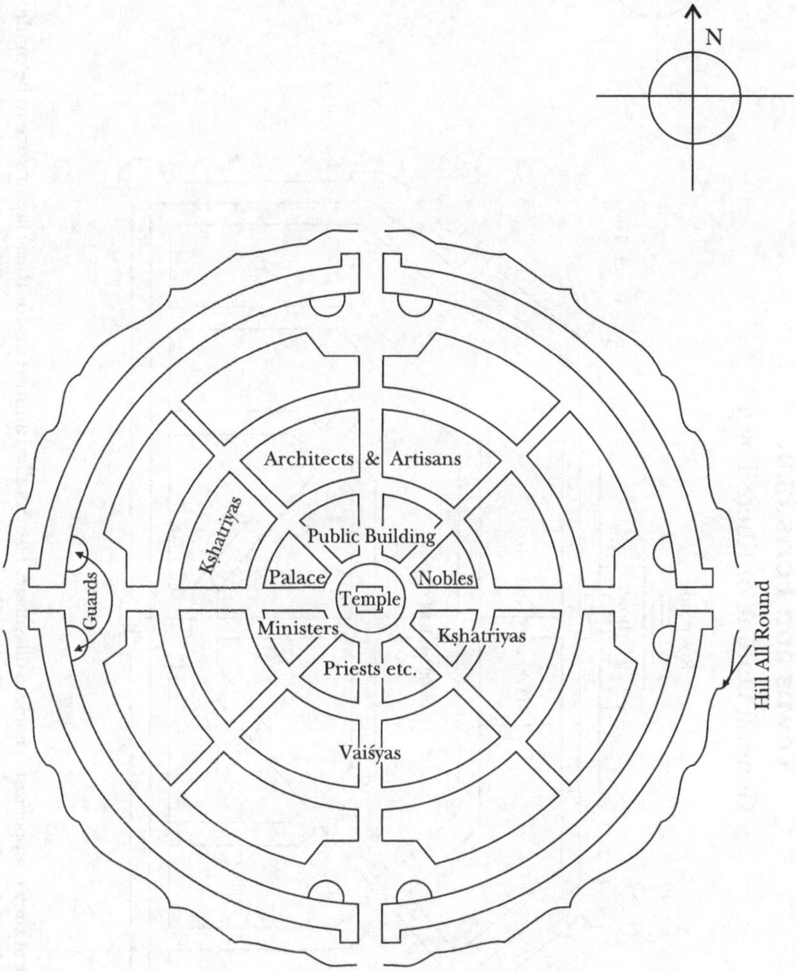

NOTE:
The detailed allotments for these layouts are to be made on the same principle on which the villages have been designed.

Towns and Forts Plan

General Outline of Kheṭa Town

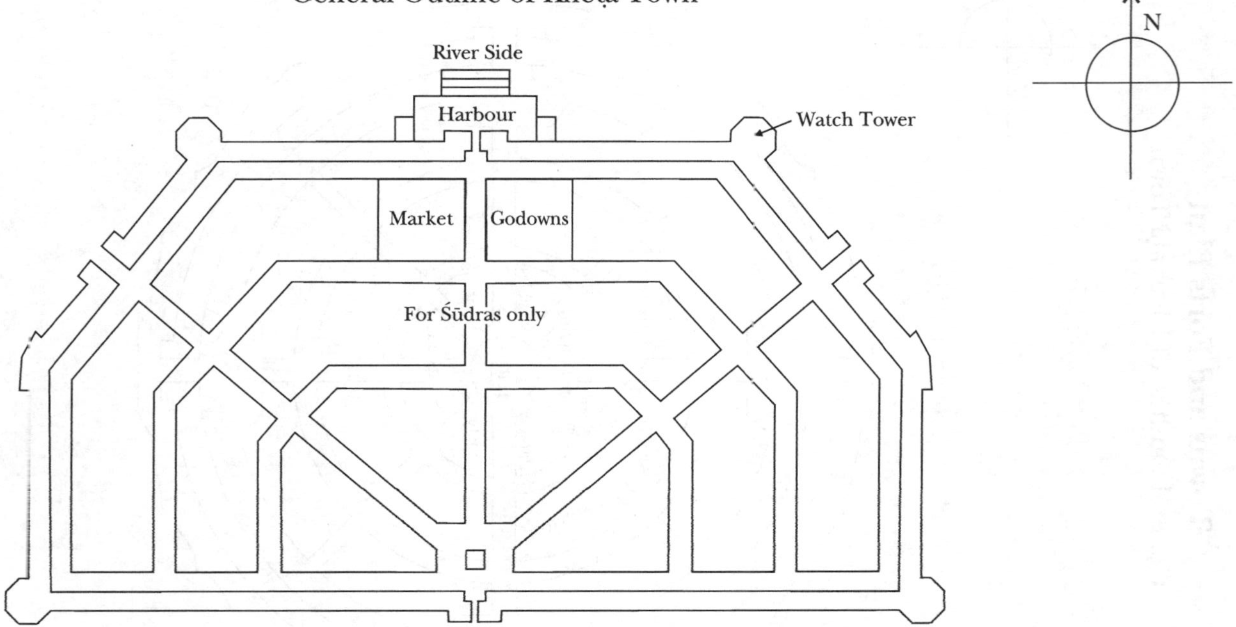

NOTE:
There should be no residence of kings or upper caste people in this village. The detailed allotments for these layouts are to be made on the same principle on which the villages have been designed.

Towns and Forts Plan

General Outline of Kubjaka Town

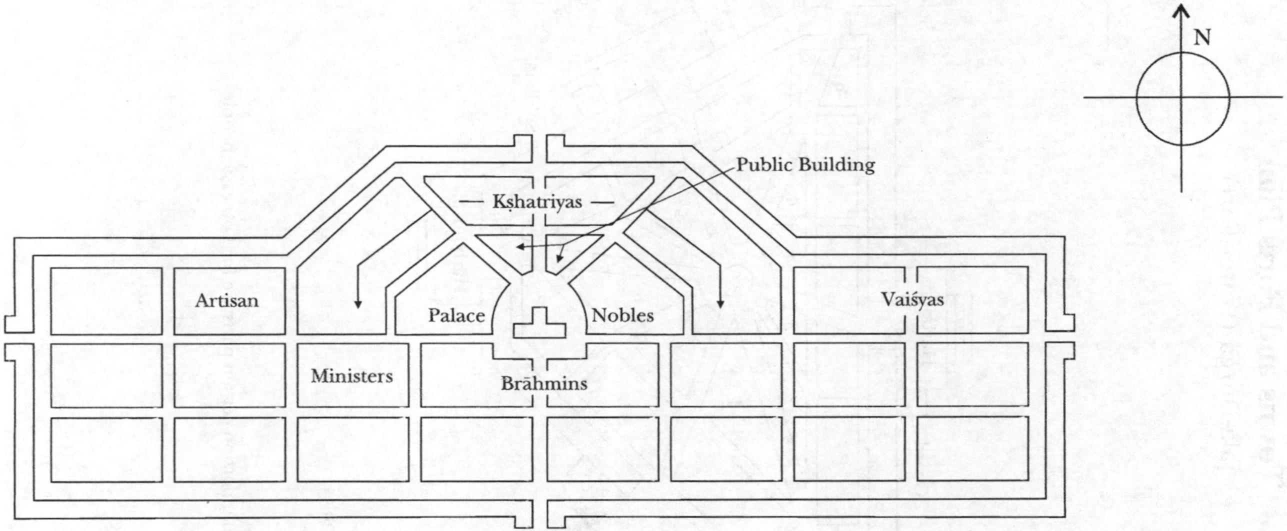

NOTE:
The detailed allotments for these layouts are to be made on the same principle on which the villages have been designed.

Towns and Forts Plan

Jala-Durga (Water-Fort)

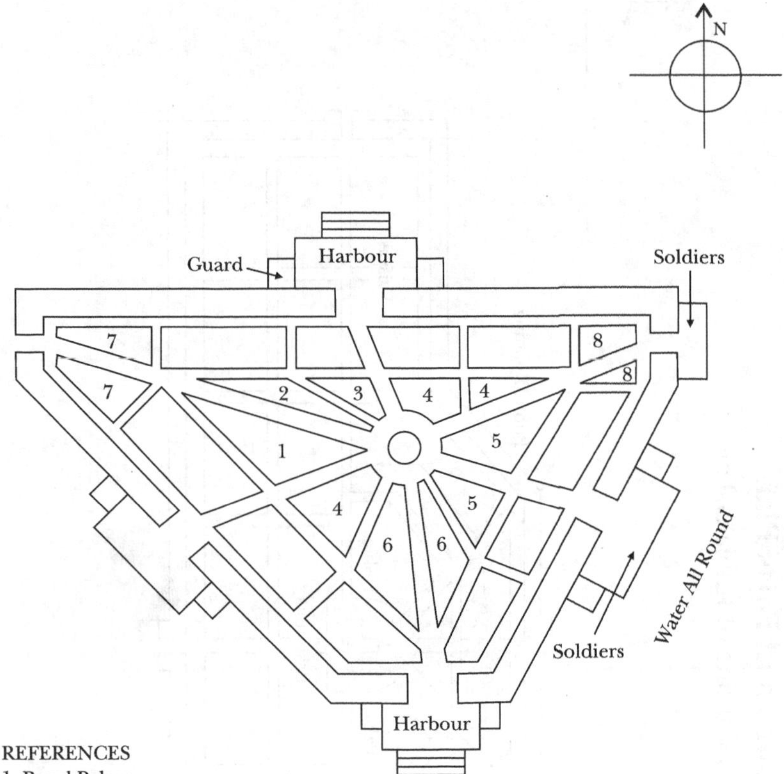

REFERENCES
1. Royal Palace
2. Ministers
3. Public Offices
4. Kṣhatriyas & Nobles
5. Brāhmins
6. Police
7-8. Armoury etc.
~ of the remaining portion certain parts are for Low-caste people

GENERAL NOTE:-
The other types of forts are not shown vary only in minor details.

Towns and Forts Plan

Droṇaka–a Fortress

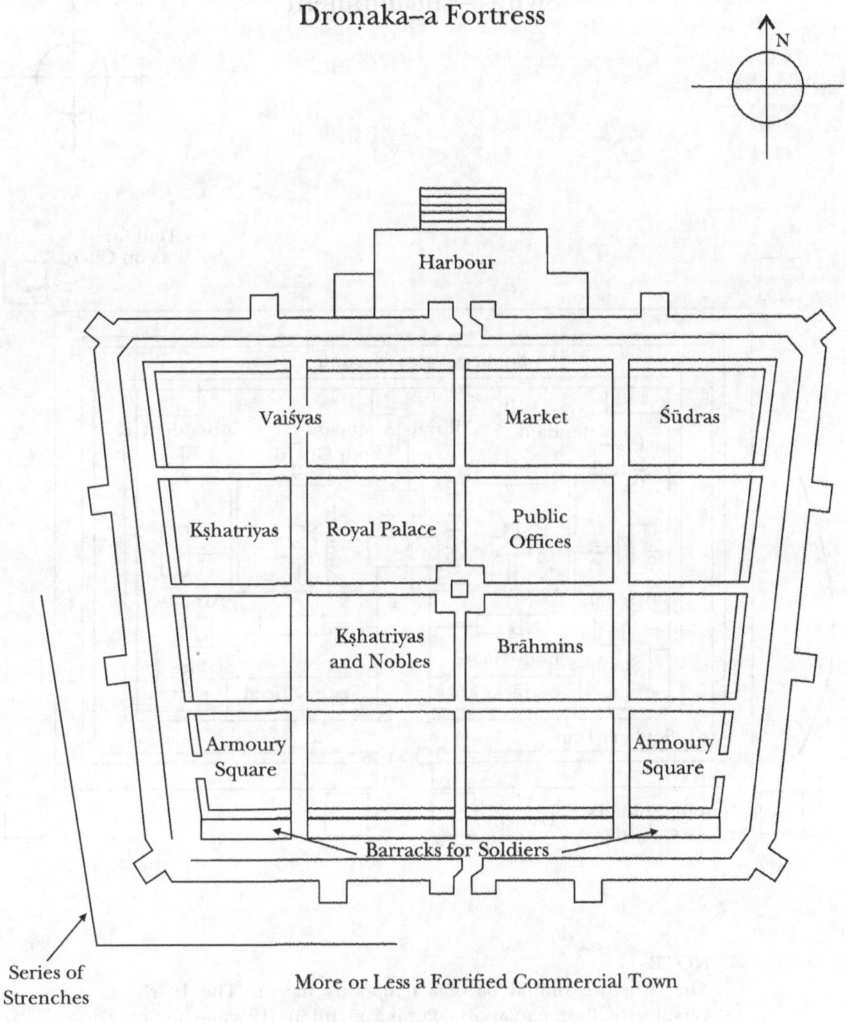

More or Less a Fortified Commercial Town

GENERAL NOTE:-

The other types of forts are not shown vary only in minor details.

Towns and Forts Plan

Sivira—Encampment

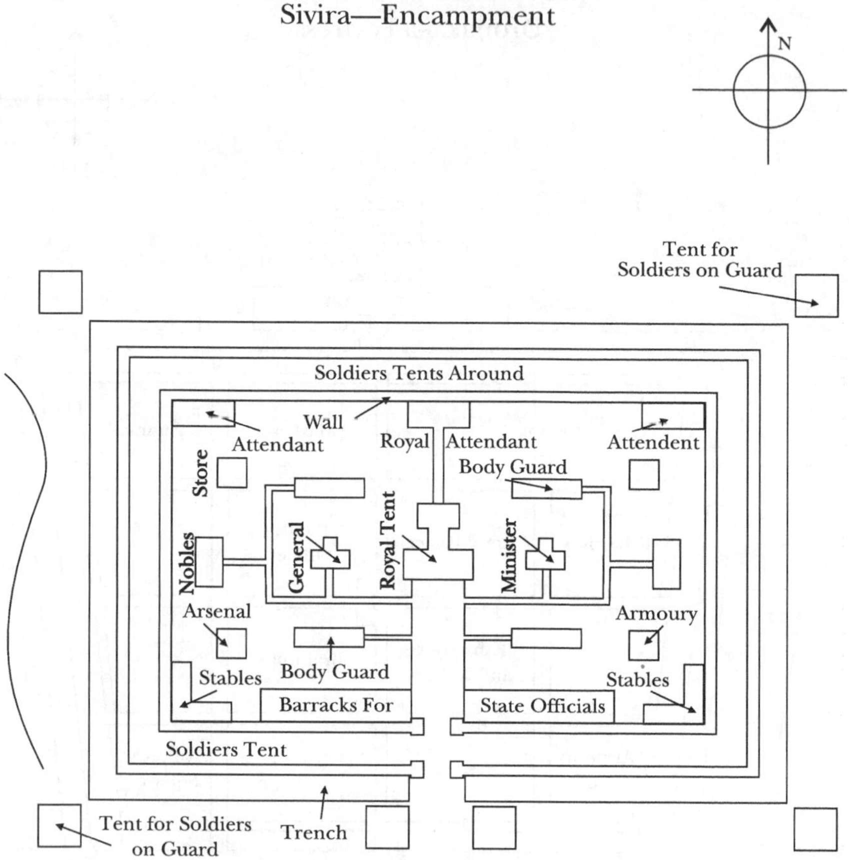

NOTE:-

The structure should be of a temporary nature. The 103rd Chapter of Brahma-Vaivarta Purāna mentions 12 gates for a Sivira but Manasara is silent on the point. So only one gate has been shown.

GENERAL NOTE:-

The other types of forts are not shown vary only in minor details.

Towns and Forts Plan

Details of Fort Gates

As obtained from Artha-Śāstra

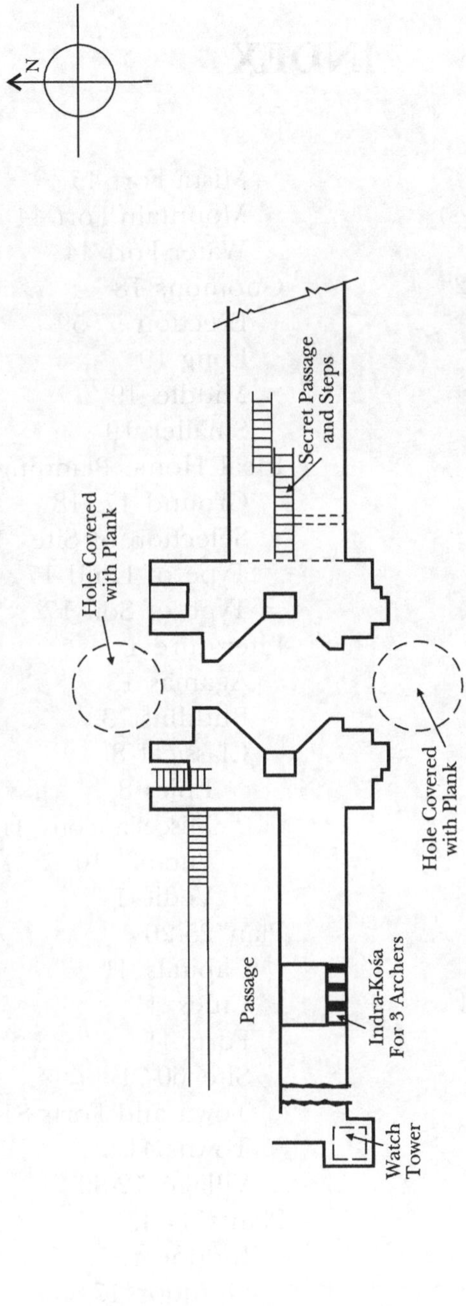

GENERAL NOTE:-
The other types of forts are not shown vary only in minor details.

INDEX